SHRINES OF
OUR LADY

SHRINES
of OUR LADY

*A guide to fifty of the world's most
famous Marian shrines*

PETER MULLEN
Foreword by JANICE T. CONNELL

ST. MARTIN'S PRESS NEW YORK

To my mother

Foreword © 1998 by Janice T. Connell

Library of Congress Cataloging-in-Publication Data (TK)

ISBN 0-312-19503-6

First published in the United States by St. Martin's Press
First published in Great Britain by Piatkus Books
First Edition: August 1998
First U.S. Edition: November 1998

10 9 8 7 6 5 4 3 2 1

Printed and bound in Great Britain by
Butler and Tanner Ltd, Frome, Somerset

HALF-TITLE PAGE *The Madonna di Ognissanti*, Ambrogio Bondone Giotto, c 1310
FRONTISPIECE *The Immaculate Conception*, Diego Rodriguez de Silva y Velasquez, c 1618

NOTE TO THE READER

SHRINES OF OUR LADY includes a selection of fifty Marian shrines from around the world. Given that there are thousands of shrines to Our Lady in every country of the world, this book cannot hope to cover them all, nor can it claim to include all the most important. There are many much loved shrines which I would have liked to include but I have had to bow to the limitations of space. Much of the information contained in this guide is sourced in the books *Meetings with Mary* and *The Visions of the Children* by Janice T. Connell. The bibliography contains additional information for those wishing to find out more about these and other important Marian shrines.

The location directions given at the end of each entry are to the town or area mentioned in the main heading rather than to the precise location of the shrine within that place. Readers should use the contact numbers provided, or local information, for further guidance. Times of services are correct at time of going to press but always check locally first to avoid disappointment. Telephone/fax numbers are for use within that particular country only. If dialing from outside the country, use the appropriate code.

ACKNOWLEDGMENTS

The author would like to thank the directors of all those shrines which generously supplied information, photographs and videos featuring their activities.

Particular thanks are also due to Janice T. Connell for valuable source material and generous support.

PICTURE CREDITS

The publishers wish to thank the following photographers and organizations for their kind permission to reproduce photographs in this book:

J. Allan Cash 20, 78, 83, 165, 174; Axiom / James Morris 116, 117; Peter V. Bianchi 171; The Bridgeman Art Library / Museo di San Marco dell'Angelico, Florence 13 / Santa Maria Gloriosa dei Frari, Venice 4 / Palazzo Ducale, Urbino 2 / Uffizi, Florence i; The Hutchison Library 82, 163 / Dave Brinicombe 41; The Irish Picture Library 100; The National Gallery London ii, vi, 49, 87; Peter Thornes 56, 57; Trip / C. Caffrey 128 / Clay Perry 54 / J. Randall 79 / A. Tovy 105; The Visual Arts Library / Louvre, Paris 10; The J. Foulston Collection 92.

Every effort has been made to trace copyright holders. However, if there are any omissions we will be happy to rectify them in future editions.

CONTENTS

The Virgin and Child, Domenico
Ghirlandaio, 1448-1494

FOREWORD
BY JANICE T. CONNELL

HERE IS A GLORIOUS book for people of the light. Jesus prayed at His Last Supper that we might all be one family, and from the cross, He gave us His Mother as our own. In these times, as never before in history, Mary, the Mother of Jesus Christ, is manifesting herself to people all over the world. Her apparitions are a magnificent gift of heaven's graciousness. But such appearances are by no means new. There is exquisite precedence for apparitions of the Blessed Virgin Mary throughout recorded history, and even before her birth on earth. Many such places where Our Lady has appeared are now famous shrines where God's people congregate for various and often quite private reasons.

This book offers visual and spiritual ways to enter deeper into the mystery of God's Plan for the human race, for every apparition of Our Lady contains divine messages we each need to hear for ourselves. Treasure this book for its timeliness and the universality of its appeal. Study the divine visitations that are presented as if each manifestation is personally for you. Then you will be happy. Then you will know how truly loved you are. Share this book with those whom you love. Then you will be a peacemaker.

Accept this book as a spiritual opportunity to experience wonderful prayers and see beautiful places. Use this book as an instrument by which you may receive a portion of God's Spirit through Mary, spouse of the Holy Spirit. "Then, whether you are young or old, you too shall see visions and dream dreams. Then will *your* sons and daughters prophesy. And God, Who works wonders in the heavens above, and signs on the earth below, shall bring forth that great and glorious day of the Lord for which we all pine." (Acts 2: 17-21)

JANICE T. CONNELL graduated from Georgetown University School of Foreign Service, earned a Masters Degree from the University of Pittsburgh Graduate School of Public and International Administration, and earned her Doctorate in Jurisprudence at Duquesne University School of Law. Married and the mother of three children, an attorney, business consultant and advisor to government and industry, Mrs Connell is considered a leading authority on Marian Spirituality. She is the author of *Queen of the Cosmos*, *The Visions of the Children*, *Triumph of the Immaculate Heart*, *Angel Power*, *Meetings with Mary*, *Praying with Mary* and *Prayer Power*.

INTRODUCTION

I T WAS A WARM spring evening on the volcanic island of Tenerife, lying west of Morocco in the Atlantic Ocean, and I was walking down through the forest from the crater under the snow-capped summit of Mount Teide. Spread out below me on the seashore lay the village of Candelaria. The promenade was lined with statues of the island's former rulers, the Guanches, and in the market square stood the ancient church. Today the place was brilliant with flowers, and the singing of choirs filled the air. The young people of the village were processing into the church for their Confirmation.

Such a scene might have been experienced at any time in rural Europe during the last thousand years. What was taking place at Candelaria was the celebration by country people of the faith which had shaped their lives for centuries. This was religion from the heart, filled not with doctrines and dogmas but with natural things and natural sounds: bells and candles, blossoms and human voices, the aromatic blend of ritual and red wine.

✤ A JOYFUL OCCASION

After the service I sat at a pavement café and fell into conversation with some local people, who told me that Candelaria is the site of a shrine of the Blessed Virgin Mary. I discovered also that every year, before the start of the university term, students from all over Tenerife make a pilgrimage here. The idea of pilgrimage suggests sacrifices, sackcloth and ashes, but for these students it is a delightful country walk across one of the most spectacular islands in the world. Their pilgrimage is a mixture of religious observance, ramble and Sunday school outing, and the cheering fact is that spirituality can be a combination of all these things.

What impressed me on my visit to Candelaria was the welcome extended to everyone – to the devout and the prayerful, but also to casual visitors and passing tourists. No one was trying to 'thrust religion down your throat', as the unfortunate saying has it. The ritual was sincere and firmly based in theology; but it also, charmingly, contained elements of a fair and a picnic. It was, in fact, the perfectly natural expression of the life of a small community.

But it was more than that. Those prayers and songs of praise were not invented in Candelaria: they are the creation of the worldwide Church, the embodiment of two thousand years of our spiritual and cultural heritage. And so as I sat there first in the village church and then at the café, I felt a sense of belonging not just to a picturesque local celebration but to a shared experience of universal significance.

A similar event, with local variations, might be witnessed at many other places throughout Europe and beyond, in Africa, the Americas, the Pacific rim and Australasia. To visit one of the great shrines of the Blessed Virgin is a magical experience, but also a very homely one: it is like coming home to mother. There is no protocol or etiquette, no examination in religious doctrines before you are allowed to join the throng. Visit one of these holy places, and you know you belong to a worldwide homely family.

✤ THE FAMILY OF OUR LADY

Families are familiar. The miracle is that the towering grandeur of the Church's teaching about Mary, the Mother of Jesus, is accompanied by a glorious informality. I remember once in Ireland I asked in a village shop where I might find the local shrine. The woman shopkeeper replied, 'Ah, 'tis just up the road you'll be lookin' for. That's where Herself appeared.' I was seized by an irresistible thought that 'Herself', the Mother of God, might have just called in for a bag of apples and a loaf of home-baked bread. You can think these things without any

suspicion of irreverence. That's what I mean by 'homely' and 'familiar'.

Of course profound religious convictions are held about the shrines. They are believed by millions to be places where the Blessed Virgin appeared to ordinary mortals – and always to the humble, usually to poor peasant folk and unschooled children. Such is the nature of divine visitation that the corridors of power in the Vatican were compelled by the witness of the fourteen-year-old Bernadette Soubirous to proclaim that the Immaculate Conception had indeed shown herself near a muddy stream on the edge of an isolated village in south-western France. Nowadays most of the world has heard of Lourdes.

So believers attend the shrines and worship there in their millions. But you are not compelled to believe the miracles before entering: indeed, visitors and tourists turn up in almost greater numbers than devout pilgrims. Why do they do so? One answer, of course, is that it is always good to go to something worth seeing. The shrines are undeniably beautiful, full of a sense of magical peace and restfulness even when they are crowded. But there is a deeper reason for this irresistible attraction: the shrines to the Virgin Mary are places where, in the words of T.S. Eliot in *Four Quartets*, 'Prayer has been valid.'

ABOVE *Madonna and Child*, Italian, School of the Marches, 15th century

THE TRUTH
THAT SETS US FREE

We live in a fast-moving world of rampant technology and frightening uncertainties. Sometimes it feels as if all the gentleness and tenderness have been squeezed out and drained away. We all have personal experience of suffering, disquiet and grief. Our brash, over-confident twentieth century has ironically also been called the Age of Anxiety.

We crave respite and rest, wholeness and inner peace. The psychologist Jung said that we desire above all things the rediscovery of the feminine – not just the concept of femininity, but a heartfelt inner tenderness and the faculty of intuition. We have lost our internal equilibrium and are increasingly forced into an existence dominated by masculine characteristics such as competition and aggressiveness. This can be soul-destroying in a literal sense – the Latin word for soul is *anima*, which is feminine.

The poet Coleridge was once asked to write a book of evidence for Christianity. He declined, saying, 'I am weary of evidences! Make people *feel* the truth, and the truth shall set them free!' One sublime painting tells us more than all the treatises on library shelves. The music of Bach, Mozart and Schubert can be a religious experience in itself.

Academics and intellectuals may regard pictures as merely symbolic of their superior world of research and ideas. The truth is the opposite: we are fundamentally creatures of feeling and tangible experience. So while

Jung may say, with the best of intentions, 'We must rediscover the feminine principle', I should like to say instead, 'Let me show you the shrines of the Blessed Virgin.' Go there and you will find answers to questions you didn't even know you were asking.

O fruitful garden, and yet never till'd!
Box full of treasure, yet by no means fill'd!
O thou which hast made Him that first
   made thee!
O near kin to all the Trinity!
O palace, where the King of all, and more,
Went in and out, yet never open'd door
Whose flesh is purer than an other spirit
Reach him our prayers, and reach us down
   His Merit!
O bread of life which swell'dst up without
   leaven!
O bridge which join'st together earth and
   heaven!
Whose eyes see me through these walls and
   through glass,
And through this flesh like as through
   cypress pass,
Behold a little heart made great by Thee,
Swelling, yet shrinking at Thy majesty.
O dwell in it! For wheresoe'er Thou go'st,
There is the temple of the Holy Ghost.

JOHN DONNE (1572–1631),
'A POEM FOR MAY'

FOLLOWING PAGE *The Assumption of the Virgin*, Titian, c 1485-1576

THE MARIAN PHENOMENON

ALL THE GOSPEL writers of the New Testament refer to Mary, the Mother of Jesus. St Luke says that she lived 'in a town of Galilee called Nazareth where she was betrothed to a man named Joseph'. Mary received a vision of the Archangel Gabriel who told her that, while she was yet a virgin, she would give birth to a son whose name would be Jesus. Mary's response to the angel is preserved in the words of the Magnificat (see p.17).

While Mary was pregnant a population census was ordered in the Roman Empire, for which purpose all heads of households had to register in the town of their birth. Joseph and Mary travelled to Bethlehem, the birthplace of Joseph, who was of the lineage of King David. Her child, the boy Jesus, was born in a stable there because, with the influx of so many visitors, there was no room for them at the inn.

The next mention of Mary in the New Testament is when Jesus was a boy of twelve and, according to custom, was taken to Jerusalem to be presented in the Temple. She was also present at Jesus's first miracle which he performed at a wedding feast in Cana, Galilee, by turning water into wine (John 2:1–11).

Throughout the ministry of Jesus, Mary remains in the background, but she stood at the foot of the Cross when He was crucified (John 19:25). Little is known about her life after the Resurrection, but St Luke records that she was among the first believers and that she witnessed the growth of the Church in Jerusalem (Acts 1:14).

So much for the bare facts of her earthly life. There are various other traditions which embellish these scanty details, and, of course, a huge devotional veneration has grown up around her over the centuries. Such traditions were frequently believed and celebrated by devout ordinary Christians for hundreds of years before the Church, ever cautious before pronouncing on such matters, declared them to be officially accepted.

✤ THE IMMACULATE CONCEPTION

The doctrine of the Immaculate Conception, described more fully on p. 83, declares that Mary was conceived by her mother, St Anne,

MARIAN YEARS

From time to time the Pope declares that a coming year shall be designated 'Marian', which means one in which particular devotions are paid to Our Lady. These years are usually in honour of a spiritual event. In recent times, 1950 was declared a Marian Year to mark the proclamation of the dogma of the Assumption, and 1954 was so designated in commemoration of the centenary of the proclamation of the Immaculate Conception (see p. 83).

and her father, St Joachim, without original sin. The associated festival is celebrated annually on 8 December.

✤ THE ASSUMPTION

At the end of her life on earth, the Church teaches, Mary was 'assumed', body and soul, into heaven. This teaching was first proclaimed by St Gregory of Tours in the sixth century. An earlier tradition has it that all the Apostles witnessed her death, but that when her tomb was opened years later it was found to be empty.

The doctrine of the Assumption was defended in the Middle Ages by St Albertus Magnus and St Thomas Aquinas. It has been adhered to by Christians from the earliest times, and eventually, on 1 November 1950, Pope Pius XII declared the Assumption of the Blessed Virgin to be an article of faith. It is celebrated annually on 15 August.

✤ MARIAN DEVOTION

Devotion to Our Lady began in the earliest years of Christianity, and she is revered in Christian literature from as early as AD 150 in *The Proto Evangelium of James*. Marian devotions which celebrated the Nativity and the Assumption were enormously popular even before they received official support from the Church authorities.

Throughout the history of the world, sites associated with any one religion have often been re-used by its successor. To do so reinforces the new religion, but may also result in the characteristics of deities of different faiths becoming intermingled. Statues of the Virgin, for instance, used to be paraded around the fields to ensure a good harvest. The moon and stars, symbols of Diana, Greco-Roman goddess of hunting were later associated with the Virgin, and Mary is frequently referred to as Stella Maris – Star of the Sea. Festivals, too, were assimilated into the new faith: the Festival of the Purification of the Blessed Virgin Mary on 2 February was originally a Roman festival

Let Mary never be far from your lips and from your heart. Following her, you will never sink into despair. Contemplating her, you will never go wrong.

ST BERNARDINO OF SIENA (1380–1444)

of purification. And Christians often took over the pagan shrines of the ancient world's goddesses and rededicated them to Mary. A good example is the shrine to Diana at Ephesus, which was re-established in the fourth century as a shrine to the Virgin.

❖ PRAYER AND LITERATURE

Since the Middle Ages many hymns and prayers have been written to Our Lady, and a number of the more interesting or important ones will be found in this book. She continues to inspire writers both secular and theological in the present day, such as T.S. Eliot and Robert Graves.

❖ MIRACLES OLD AND NEW

Since the early days of the Christian Church the Virgin has been credited with the working of miracles of healing and conversion, which is why the shrines that this book describes were created. Those miracles reflect her intercessionary role as a being who spans heaven and earth: Christ is the judge, whose anger His mother softens. For this reason, since the ninth century she has been referred to as the Mediatrix. In many of the visions described in this book Mary is perceived as pleading to God on behalf of sinners.

In the twentieth century the number of apparitions of Mary has greatly increased. Our Lady has typically revealed herself to poor and humble people, and calls for prayer and for the rejection of violence and materialism. The clear warnings in some of her messages have given rise to a belief that the increased

number of visions is a sign that the end of the world is approaching and that Christians should prepare for the Second Coming of Christ.

❖ PSYCHOLOGY AND THE FEMININE PRINCIPLE

Biblical Christianity is a very masculine affair in which God the Father, Son and Holy Spirit are imagined as male characters (though an old tradition speaks of the Holy Spirit as

---

FURTHER TITLES OF MARY

Throughout Christian history and tradition more than 170 titles have been given to Our Lady. Some of these are explained in the text; others include:

Mother of God: this traditional title is somewhat misleading, for it is derived from a Greek word meaning 'the one who gave birth to God'. But in this context 'God' refers to Jesus

Queen of Peace: the title used by Pope Benedict XV to address the Virgin during the First World War (1914–18), when fierce fighting raged throughout Europe and beyond

Exemplar: a title confirmed by the Second Vatican Council (1962–5), which declared that Mary is a perfect example to us of the virtues of faith, hope and love

---

feminine). But many of the older pagan religions were female-based, with mother goddesses associated in particular with fertility and the seasons. When Christianity supplanted these faiths, the veneration of the Virgin Mary filled the void and provided a balance between male and female.

Theologians have had much to say about the role of the Blessed Virgin in the redemption of the world, but the feminine principle has also been emphasized by many great writers in the history of Western civilization. In *The Divine Comedy* the medieval Italian poet Dante ascribes to his ideal woman, Beatrice, and then to the Virgin, powers of intercession and redemption. Goethe comes close to saying that the total responsibility for the salvation of the world is left to the feminine principle – to the character he describes as '*Das Ewig-Weibliche*', variously translated as the Endless Woman-Soul, the Eternal Feminine or the Ever-Womanly.

The most important secular writer on the need to restore the masculine–feminine balance was the great psychologist Carl Gustav Jung (1875–1961), who asserted that it is psychologically necessary for us to accept the divinity of the feminine. Robert Graves's *The White Goddess* is a profound study of the place of the eternal feminine in Western civilization.

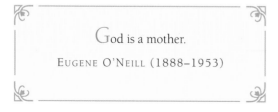

God is a mother.

EUGENE O'NEILL (1888–1953)

❖ MUSIC

The ancient hymns to the Virgin Mary have been set to music since medieval times and are known as *The Antiphons of the Blessed Virgin Mary*. Many of them were set in the early musical form known as plainsong. Many sixteenth-century composers, including Palestrina (1525–94), William Byrd (1543–1623) and Thomas Tallis (1505–85) wrote settings of the antiphons in a particularly rich period in the history of Church music. One particularly famous setting of a Marian theme is Monteverdi's *Vespers of the Virgin Mary* of 1610.

The *Magnificat* of Johann Sebastian Bach (1685–1750) is an acknowledged masterpiece. The eighteenth- and early nineteenth-century composers Haydn (1732–1809), Mozart (1756–91) and Schubert (1797–1828) wrote scores of settings of such favourite devotions as the *Ave Maria* and *Salve Regina*. Haydn and Mozart were not unusual in having, at some stage in their lives, religious patrons who would have commissioned such works. In the Romantic period, Berlioz (1803–69) composed a beautiful oratorio called *L'Enfance du Christ*.

Explicitly religious music, like religious painting, has gone out of fashion in the twentieth entury. Nevertheless there are still a few composers, such as John Taverner, born in 1944, who have produced music on a Marian theme.

The Virgin Mary also, of course, has her part in the Mass. There are magnificent settings of the *Et Incarnatus Est* by composers from the time of Bach to the present day.

Nor should we forget the wealth of Marian musical devotion to be found in the hymn books of both the Catholic and Anglican Churches.

ART AND SYMBOL

Various symbols and emblems are typically associated with Mary. The lily denotes purity and the unicorn chastity, since according to traditional belief the creature can only sleep in the lap of a virgin. The Virgin is often depicted and described as a Lily among Thorns, an image whose symbolism is obvious. The colour white, symbolizing divine light and purity, is also frequently encountered in descriptions or representations of the Virgin. So is blue, representing heaven. Stars, an attribute borrowed from a pagan deity, have already been referred to. All these elements and others are to be encountered in the vast body of Western religious art which depicts scenes in the life of the Virgin.

In the early years of Christianity, icons and paintings frequently featured the Madonna and Child. There was a definite religious purpose behind this particular image: it was intended to underpin the idea of the Incarnation – that God is with us in the person of Jesus.

Our Lady was believed to be the Queen of Heaven, and in Byzantine art she was pictured as such, seated on the royal cushion and throne. An early example of this image is a sixth-century mosaic at Parenzo in Italy. She may also be seen as Queen with the Christ Child on her lap in the famous *Nikopeia* installed in St Mark's, Venice, in 1204.

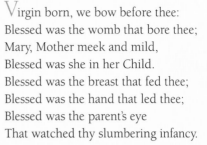

Virgin born, we bow before thee:
Blessed was the womb that bore thee;
Mary, Mother meek and mild,
Blessed was she in her Child.
Blessed was the breast that fed thee;
Blessed was the hand that led thee;
Blessed was the parent's eye
That watched thy slumbering infancy.

Blessed she by all creation,
Who brought forth the world's salvation,
And blessed they – forever blest,
Who love thee most and serve thee best.
Virgin born, we bow before thee:
Blessed was the womb that bore thee;
Mary, Mother meek and mild,
Blessed was she in her Child.

REGINALD HEBER (1783–1826)

The Virgin at prayer, without the Christ Child, was popular in the Middle Ages. In some of the icons and paintings of this time she is pictured with a medallion bearing the image of the Infant Jesus. Again, there are examples in St Mark's.

In the fourteenth century there was a strong tradition of simple, lively images such as those produced by Lorenzetti. The famous Florentine fresco painter Giotto painted naturalistic images of Our Lady making human gestures in earthly situations. In the fifteenth century Mary was often portrayed in a garden, which was meant to symbolize her virginity, as in Lochner's *Virgin in the Rose Bower*. Another popular representation of this time was the Madonna with a Rosary.

The classical style of the Madonna and Child was perfected in the Renaissance by Raphael (1483–1520), for instance in his *Madonna del Granduca* in the Pitti Palace in Florence. At this time the Virgin and Child were often depicted talking to saints and apostles; this style became known as *Sacra Conversazione*, and a good example is the *Madonna of Victory* by Mantegna.

Our Lady was often credited with bringing relief from disease and so the image of Mary the Healer was popular, particularly in the sixteenth and seventeenth centuries. Guido Reni's *Paliotto del Voto* is a masterpiece of this kind. This image is closely related to Mary, Protectress of the People, in which she is often seen sheltering Christians under her cloak.

The doctrine of the Immaculate Conception was pictured as early as the twelfth century, and can be seen in a thirteenth-century window at Chartres Cathedral. A painting of this subject done in 1619 by the Spanish artist Velasquez showed the Virgin standing on a crescent moon in the heavens, ringed by stars.

The image of the suffering Virgin, with the body of Christ in her arms or at her feet, is known as a *Pietá*. Perhaps the best-known example is a marble statue by Michelangelo, but it has been used by many other artists including Bellini in the Renaissance and, in the nineteenth century, the French artist Delacroix.

The Virgin of the Victory, Mantegna, 1496

Series of scenes in the life of the Virgin was another popular theme, and one of the best examples can be seen in Giotto's frescoes in the Scoregni Chapel at Padua in Italy. Of all the events in Our Lady's life, none has been painted more often than the Annunciation: that painted by Botticelli (c.1445–1510) is perhaps the most famous. The Assumption was painted widely from the twelfth century onwards. Some early sixteenth-century woodcuts by the German artist Albrecht Dürer (1471–1528) are an outstanding example, and show the Virgin being crowned by the Holy Trinity. Possibly the most magnificent *Assumption* is the one by the Venetian artist Titian (c.1487–1576) in the Church of Santa Maria Gloriosa dei Frari in Venice.

Even in modern, more secular times the image of a mother and child often takes on religious overtones. The twentieth-century sculptors Jacob Epstein and Henry Moore both produced work of this kind, emphasizing the universal nature of the Virgin as the symbol of perfect womanhood that transcends individual cultures and religious beliefs.

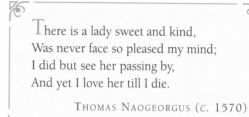

There is a lady sweet and kind,
Was never face so pleased my mind;
I did but see her passing by,
And yet I love her till I die.

THOMAS NAOGEORGUS (C. 1570)

MAJOR FESTIVALS OF THE VIRGIN

2 February: Purification of the Blessed Virgin Mary: marks the presentation of the boy Jesus in the Temple at Jerusalem

25 March: Annunciation of the Blessed Virgin Mary: marks the occasion when the Archangel Gabriel announced to Mary that she would bear a son and call him Jesus

31 May: Visitation of the Blessed Virgin Mary: marks the occasion of Mary's visit to her cousin Elizabeth

15 August: Assumption of the Blessed Virgin Mary: marks the taking up of the Virgin, body and soul, into heaven

8 September: Nativity of Our Lady: the Virgin's birthday

8 December: Immaculate Conception: marks the day when the Virgin was conceived by her mother, St Anne

PRAYERS OF OUR LADY

MANY PRAYERS have been written to invoke the aid of the Virgin Mary. Here are some of the more famous ones. Others, such as the Prayer to Our Lady of Evesham, will be found with the description of the relevant shrine.

AVE MARIA ✤ HAIL MARY

THIS IS THE most famous of all the ancient prayers to the Virgin and was probably being recited by Christians from the beginning. It is known as the Angelic Salutation because it is based on words which the Angel Gabriel spoke to Mary at the Annunciation as recorded in the first chapter of St Luke's gospel. The Ave Maria was authorized by the Church and entered in the Breviary of Pope Pius V in 1568.

One of the most reassuring aspects of this prayer is the fact that the rhythm of the Latin original is preserved in the English version. So the modern pilgrim who prays these ancient words is praying just as the early Christians prayed. And so we belong to a tradition which reaches back to the earliest years of the faith. Ancient and modern: everyone is singing the same song.

Ave Maria, gratia plena, Dominus tecum; benedicta tu in mulieribus, et benedictus fructus ventris tui, Jesus. Sancta Maria, Mater Dei, ora pro nobis peccatoribus, nunc et in hora mortis nostrae. Amen.

Hail Mary, full of grace: the Lord is with thee. Blessed art thou among women, and blessed is the fruit of thy womb, Jesus. Holy Mary, Mother of God, pray for us sinners now and at the hour of our death. Amen.

Regina Coeli ✣ O Queen of Heaven

This is the Easter Anthem to the Blessed Virgin and it was probably composed in the twelfth century, although an ancient tradition says that it was written by Pope Gregory V around 998 AD.

Regina Coeli, laetare, alleluia. Quia quem meruisti portare, alleluia.
Resurrexit sicut dixit, alleluia. Ora pro nobis Deum, alleluia.
Gaude et laetare, Virgo Maria, alleluia.
Quia surrexit Dominus vere, alleluia!

Joy to thee, O Queen of Heaven! Alleluia.
He whom thou wast fit to bear, alleluia.
As He promised, hath arisen, alleluia.
Pour for us to God thy prayer, alleluia.
Rejoice and be glad, O Virgin Mary, alleluia.
For the Lord hath risen indeed, alleluia!

The Annunciation, Fra Angelico, c 1438-45

Ave Maris Stella ✦ Hail Star of the Sea

THIS IS ONE of the most ancient and popular of all the hymns of Mary, dating from the eighth century. It has a simple, beautiful rhythm and is a tender hymn which asks for the motherly help of the Blessed Virgin.

Ave, maris stella,
Dei Mater Alma,
Atque semper Virgo,
Felix coeli porta.

Hail, thou star of ocean,
Portal of the sky,
Ever Virgin Mother,
Of the Lord most high.

Sumens illud Ave
Gabrielis ore
Funda nos in pace,
Mutans Hevac nomen

O by Gabriel's Ave
Uttered long ago
Eva's name reversing,
Peace confirm below.

Solve vincla reis,
Profer lumen caecis,
Mala nostra pelle,
Bona cuncta posce.

Break the captive's fetters,
Light on blindness pour;
Chase all evils from us,
Every bliss implore.

Monstra te esse matrem
Sumat per te preces
Qui pro nobis natus
Tulit esse tuus

Show thyself a Mother,
Offer Him our sighs,
Who for us incarnate
Did not thee despise.

Virgo singularis,
Inter omnes mitis,
Nos culpis solutos
Mites fac et castos.

Virgin all excelling,
Passing meek and lowly,
Freed from guilt preserve us
Blameless chaste and holy.

Vitam praesta puram
Iter para tutum:
Ut videntes Jesum
Semper collaetemur.

Still as on we journey
Help our weak endeavour
Till we gaze on Jesus
And rejoice forever.

Sit laos Deo Patri,
Summo Christo decus,
Spiritui Sancto,
Tribus honor unus.

Father, Son and Spirit,
Three in one confessing
Give we equal glory
Equal praise and blessing.

Amen

Amen

THE HOLY ROSARY

THIS IS THE most famous and popular of all the devotions to the Virgin Mary. It was written by St Dominic in 1206 after a vision in which the Blessed Virgin gave him the Rosary. The intention was originally a series of prayers against the Albigensian or Cathar heresy of the twelfth century. According to this heresy, Christ was an angel with a phantom body. This is the very opposite of the teaching of the New Testament which declares firmly that Christ was 'made flesh' and that he was truly human. He became like us so that he could save us from our sins.

So the Rosary emphasizes physical and fleshly aspects of the Christian faith, such as the birth, suffering, death and resurrection of Jesus Christ. The beads are an aid to memory and concentration through the cycle, which consists of one Our Father, one Gloria and ten Hail Marys repeated fifteen times in commemoration of the Joyful, Sorrowful and Glorious Mysteries of Our Lord.

The five Joyful Mysteries
the Annunciation, the Visitation, the Nativity, the Presentation and the Finding of the Boy Jesus in the Temple.

The five Sorrowful Mysteries
Jesus's Prayer at Gethsemane, His Scourging, the Crown of Thorns, the Carrying of the Cross and the Crucifixion.

The five Glorious Mysteries
the Resurrection, the Ascension, the coming of the Holy Spirit, the Assumption of the Virgin Mary into Heaven and the Coronation of the Virgin Mary.

THE ANGELUS

THIS POPULAR devotion, composed in the twelfth century, is said traditionally three times a day: early morning, noon and evening. The angelus bell is rung and then priest and people join in this commemoration of the Annunciation, when the Angel Gabriel told Mary that she was to bear the infant Jesus.

Angelus Domini nuntiavit Mariae. Et concepit de Spiritu Sancto.

Ave Maria . . .

Ecce ancilla Domini. Fiat mihi secundum verbum tuum.

Ave Maria . . .

Et verbum caro factum est. Et habitavit in nobis.

Ave Maria . . .

Ora pro nobis, sancta Dei Genitrix. Ut digni efficiamur promissionibus Christi.

The Angel of the Lord declared unto Mary, and she conceived of the Holy Ghost.

Hail Mary . . .

Behold the handmaid of the Lord;

Be it done unto me according to thy Word.

Hail Mary . . .

And the Word was made flesh and dwelt among us.

Hail Mary . . .

Holy Mother of God, pray for us,

That we may be made worthy of the promises of Christ.

THE MAGNIFICAT

THIS IS THE exultant prayer of the Virgin Mary after her vision of the Angel Gabriel, who told her that she would bear a son and call him Jesus. It is found in St Luke's Gospel 1 : 46–55 and has been one of the great prayers of the Church for almost two thousand years.

My soul magnifies the Lord,

And my spirit has rejoiced in God my Saviour.

For He has regarded the lowliness of his handmaiden,

  And, behold, from henceforth all generations shall call me blessed.

For He that is mighty has done to me great things

  And His name is holy.

His mercy is on those who fear Him, from generation to generation.

He has shown strength with His arm,

  And scattered the proud in the imagination of their hearts.

He has put down the mighty from their seat

  And exalted the humble and the meek.

He has filled the hungry with good things,

  But the rich He has sent empty away.

He has helped His servant Israel,

As He promised to our forefathers

  Abraham and his children forever.

THE AKATHIST HYMN

THIS IS attributed to St Romanos (d. 556) in Constantinople. It is the most popular of Marian devotions in the Byzantine Rite, and is notable for its profundity of thought. It begins like this.

Rejoice, through you joy rings out again.

Rejoice, through you sorrow is put to flight.

Rejoice, O resurrection of fallen Adam,

Rejoice, O redemption of the tears of Eve.

Rejoice, O sublime peak of human intellect.

Rejoice, O profound abyss even for Angel eyes.

Rejoice, for in you the King's throne was elevated.

Rejoice, for you bear the One who sustains everything.

Rejoice, O star that goes before the sun.

Rejoice, O womb of the incarnate God.

Rejoice, for through you all creation is renewed.

Rejoice, for through you the Creator became a baby.

Rejoice, O Virgin and Bride!

SALVE REGINA ✦ HAIL, HOLY QUEEN

THIS IS A popular plainsong hymn written in the eleventh century. St Bernard of Clairvaux said that the Salve Regina was the hymn of the shrine of Le Puy-en-Velay in France. This anthem has been used by the Cistercian Order since the early thirteenth century, and the 1568 Breviary of Pope Pius V declared that it should be recited after the late evening office of Compline.

Salve Regina, Mater misericordiae; Vita, dulcedo, et spes nostra, salve. Ad te clamamus, exsules filii Hevac. Ad te suspiramus, gementes et flentes in hac lacrymarum valle. Eia ergo, Advocata nostra, Illos tuos misericordes oculos ad nos converte: Et Jesum, benedictum fructum ventris tui. Nobis post hoc exsilium ostende.

O clemens, o pia, o dulcis Virgo Maria.

Hail, holy Queen, Mother of mercy; hail our life, our sweetness and our hope. To thee do we cry, poor banished children of Eve; to thee do we send up our sighs, mourning and weeping in this vale of tears. Turn then, most gracious Advocate, thine eyes of mercy towards us; and after this our exile, show unto us the blessed fruit of thy womb, Jesus. O clement, O loving, O sweet Virgin Mary.

THE
SHRINES

The Blessed Virgin
directs to us all acts that every
mother lavishes on her children.
She loves us, watches
over us, protects us and
intercedes for us.

POPE JOHN XXIII (1881–1963)

OPPOSITE The basilica of the Rosary, Lourdes, France

—— ARGENTINA ——

MARY OF THE ROSARY

SAN NICOLAS

Undoubtedly, this event of grace will continue to grow. It has proved its validity
by its spiritual fruits.

DOMINGO CASTAGNA, BISHOP OF SAN NICOLAS, 25 JULY 1990

ON 25 SEPTEMBER 1983 Gladys do Motta, a middle-aged, working-class woman with a steelworker husband and two grown-up daughters, was at home in San Nicolas, saying her prayers, when she was startled to see her rosary glow vivid red like molten metal. She called in her neighbours and they too saw the phenomenon. In the weeks that followed, Gladys prayed more devoutly and organized a small devotional group among her friends. Then one day, while she was praying the rosary alone in her room, the Blessed Virgin, holding the Infant Jesus, appeared before her. The apparition remained for some minutes without speaking and then departed as suddenly as it had come.

On 28 September the vision appeared again, and Our Lady seemed to be holding out her own rosary for Gladys to take. When on 5 October the Virgin appeared for the third time, Gladys wondered why she of all people should have been singled out to receive such mysterious manifestations. She told no one about them at that stage.

On 7 October, the Feast Day of the Holy Rosary, the Virgin appeared yet again, and this time Gladys asked what service she might perform for her. The vision made no reply, but an image of a shrine came into Gladys's mind and she interpreted it as a sign that the Virgin desired a building in her honour.

✦ YOU WILL WALK A LONG ROAD

Gladys was confused and uneasy. How could she, a poor, uneducated woman, achieve this? She decided to break her silence and to tell her priest, Father Perez, about the visions. He told her to continue faithful in prayer and regular in receiving the Blessed Sacrament. On 13 October the Virgin actually spoke to Gladys: 'You have been faithful. Don't be frightened. Come and see me. Let me take your hand and you will walk a long road.' Our Lady asked Gladys to read Ezekiel 2:4: 'They are impudent children and stiff-hearted. I send thee unto them and thou shalt say unto them, "Thus saith the Lord God".'

On 17 October, Gladys made the short journey to the cathedral in Rosario. When she went there again on the 25th the Virgin appeared to her while she knelt in prayer and said, 'Accept this rosary from my hand and treasure it for all time. You have been obedient and your obedience pleases me. Rejoice, for God is with you!'

Over the next few weeks the Virgin appeared almost every day, and Gladys also had visions of Christ who told her, 'I am the sower. Gather the harvest, for it will be plentiful.' She wrote down all that the apparitions conveyed to her and confided in Father Perez. He told her of the existence of a life-size wooden statue of Our Lady of the Rosary, which had been blessed by Pope Leo XIII and brought to Argentina from Rome in the 1880s. During a procession one of the hands had been broken. For some reason it had not been repaired, and the statue was now stored in the belfry of Rosario Cathedral. When Father Perez took Gladys to see it she exclaimed: 'This is exactly the Lady I see!' The figure was clothed in a blue dress and a pink tunic. As Gladys stood before it, the Virgin herself appeared and said, 'They have kept me in obscurity, but I have returned. Set me up again, since you see me as I am.'

✦ YOU MUST STAY AWAKE!

Gladys stood before the apparition for several minutes, convinced that the Virgin would speak again. Eventually, Our Lady said, 'I desire to stand on the bank of the Parana River. Do not lose your strength. Glory be to the Father Most High!'

In a further series of visitations, the Virgin told Gladys exactly where she desired her shrine to be built. On 24 November, Gladys and her prayer group went to the site and pondered how they could possibly raise enough money to build a shrine. The Virgin directed Gladys to read Exodus 25 : 8: 'And let them make me a sanctuary; that I may dwell among them.'

The Virgin spoke to Gladys again on 21 December and told her not to keep secret the things that she had seen and heard. A few days later she issued a warning: 'The human race is contaminated and people do not know what they want. This gives opportunity to the Devil, but he will not be the victor. Jesus Christ will triumph in the great battle. You must stay awake. I am asking you for much prayer and obedience, for the sake of the whole world. Announce this to them! Amen.'

Meanwhile Gladys had begun a strict fast, taking only fruit juice, coffee and milk. All this time the Virgin appeared to her each day.

✦ THE HEALING OF GONZALO'S TUMOUR

The Virgin had asked for a great increase in devotion, and so the rosary was said constantly in the cathedral. In October 1984 a local woman, Maria de Miguel, knelt to say the rosary on behalf of her seven-year-old son Gonzalo who had a brain tumour.

After his condition deteriorated, on 30 October he was anointed and received his First Communion. Within an hour he looked much better. A few days later doctors examined him and reported, astonished, that the tumour was now a third of its former size. Three weeks later, it had disappeared completely. News of this cure spread throughout the region, and then on 2 June 1985 the Buenos Aires newspaper *La Nacion* carried a full report.

In her prayers and fasting Gladys felt in her own body the sufferings of Christ, and she received the stigmata, the marks of Christ's wounds. The new Bishop of San Nicolas, Domingo Castagna, asked two eminent doctors to give her medical care.

At about this time the Virgin asked Gladys to remind people of her presence among them: 'Make a medal with my image. On one side it should say, "Mary of the Rosary of San Nicolas" and on the other it should display the Blessed Trinity and Seven Stars.' Since 1986 this medal has been widely distributed.

Early in 1985, Bishop Castagna gathered all the reports from Gladys concerning her visions and all the signed documents claiming miraculous cures, and set up an official commission of inquiry.

The first conclusions of the commission were published on 25 October 1985: since some of Gonzalo de Miguel's medical papers could not be found, it was not possible to say for certain that a supernatural cure had taken place. But the commissioners noted that reliable evidence suggested a miracle had indeed occurred.

✤ THE SHRINE IS BUILT

On 25 February 1986, Bishop Castagna celebrated Mass on the banks of the Parana River at the site chosen by the Virgin. He led a procession to testify to the validity of the visions, and announced that on 25 September a foundation stone would be laid on a plot of land provided by the town council. Money for the shrine was raised by public donations.

In 1987 Pope John Paul II visited the new shrine and listened to the story of Gladys's experiences. Thousands of pilgrims began to converge there regularly and many more cures were reported. On 11 February 1990 Gladys received her final visitation and message from the Blessed Virgin, who said, 'Pray constantly. Show penitence and do penance. Those who have faith in God and in me shall be saved.'

On the 25th of every month, there is a commemorative Mass presided over by the Bishop. San Nicolas pilgrims are renowned for their great intensity of prayer and devotion, and many experience vividly Our Lord's presence in the Eucharist. A Book of Testimonies is displayed in the Sanctuary. It contains almost 200 pages of personal claims of miraculous healing through prayer to Our Lady of the Rosary.

Information for Visitors

Location: 160 miles/250 km NW of Buenos Aires and just S of Rosario.
Contact Numbers: TEL/FAX (0461) 22471 or TEL (0461) 21699 .
Times of Services: call for details.

— AUSTRALIA —

OUR LADY OF MERCY

PENROSE PARK, BERRIMA

Berrima – a little town
Lost somewhere amidst the bush.
You would drive straight past without a second thought
If the name was not known to you.
ADAM GAJKOWSKI, 'BERRIMA, PENROSE PARK'

FATHER AUGUSTINE LAZUR is said by his parishioners to be 'as stubborn as a wombat'. He was born Joseph Lazur in 1931 in the village of Kondraty in Poland. In his teens he worked by day as a cook for the Carmelites and in the evenings attended classes, where he took two courses each year for seven years. When he was twenty-three Joseph entered the Pauline monastery at Jasna Gora and took the name Augustine. He continued his theological education in Warsaw and Cracow and was ordained priest in 1961. For the next twenty years he ministered in parishes in Poland, Croatia and, for eleven years, in the USA.

Augustine had always venerated the image of the Black Madonna (see p. 135) at Jasna Gora. Towards the end of the 1970s he felt an overpowering call to minister in Australia and to establish a shrine of the Virgin there. Although the General Curia of Jasna Gora

gave him permission to go, Augustine could not find an Australian sponsor to provide him with the necessary immigration credentials. All his letters to Australian dioceses were returned with the same message: 'We have no need of a Polish priest!'

✧ THE ARCHBISHOP CATCHES HIS BUS

One day Augustine was in the bus station in Rome when he was approached by a man in a cassock who was looking for the ticket-office. Augustine took the stranger there and, as they walked, the man explained that he was a visitor from Australia. Augustine told him his story and asked, 'Will you be my sponsor?' The priest replied, 'Write to me.' He turned out to be the Archbishop of Canberra.

Augustine eventually arrived in Australia in April 1981. The Archbishop appointed him

The image of the Black Madonna inside the church at Penrose Park

assistant priest at the church of Our Lady of Fatima in the town of Goulborn, and asked him to establish a shrine to the Blessed Virgin. Later Augustine was appointed to the parish of Berrima, which contained the ruins of one of the earliest Catholic churches south of Sydney. It had been built by convicts in 1849, but because the population moved away it fell into disuse and was eventually closed in 1974. Augustine and his team set about its reconstruction.

✤ A POLISH CHRISTMAS DOWN UNDER

When the work was complete, Augustine set off for Jasna Gora to bring back a large copy of the Miraculous Picture of Our Lady, which had been purchased for the proposed shrine in Berrima by the local Koncewicz family. This picture had been blessed by Pope John Paul II on his second pilgrimage to his native Poland. On 13 May 1984, the image of the

Black Madonna was processed into the church at Berrima. Finding a permanent home for the icon became a major priority.

After raising thousands of dollars through donations, Augustine purchased Berrima Farm, Penrose Park, where he founded the first Australian branch of his Order of Pauline Fathers.

Augustine discovered a huge cave in the rock on the far reaches of the Penrose Park estate. Friends of the Pauline Fathers had found statues of Our Lady of Lourdes and St Bernadette in an old orphanage, and it was decided to make them the centrepiece of a Marian centre in the cave. Pilgrimages began in 1988, and in the same year the Penrose Park, shrine was visited by the Primate of Poland, Cardinal Glemp.

✢ OUR LADY OF MERCY

From these small beginnings, pilgrims arriving at Penrose Park will now find a large square monastery which can house 15 monks. Flowing out from the monastery is a church which has seats for 600 and standing room for a further 800. Up to 40,000 pilgrims visit the shrine annually and there is a programme of special devotions throughout the year. Every month, on the thirteenth day, Our Lady of Fatima is honoured by mass with a special celebrant. The first Saturday in the month is celebrated in honour of Our Lady's request to make reparation to Her Immaculate Heart. The first and last Friday of each month is kept by an all night vigil with devotions, Exposition of the blessed Sacrament and Mass.

BLACK MADONNAS

As noted in varions places in this book, many of the so-called Black Madonnas were not black to begin with but were darkened by centuries of exposure to the atmosphere and to candle-smoke. But there is a definite tradition of Black Madonnas, notably in the Auvergne district of France where Madonnas are said to be 'black' even when they are white. These may be either statues or icons. They derive from earlier classical and pagan civilizations, and sometimes a figure of Mary has been a straight replacement for that of a classical goddess. The statue of Diana at Ephesus, for example, is widely believed to have originally been black.

Information for Visitors

Location: Penrose Park is 12 miles/19 km S of Berrima, which is 80 miles/130 km S of Sydney. **Contact Numbers:** Tel (2) 4878 9192 192 Fax (2) 4878 9351. **Times of Services:** at the shrine of the old cave, Penrose Park: weekdays 11 a.m., Sundays 9 a.m., 11 a.m. and 1 p.m.; Fatima Day (13th of each month) 11 a.m. Mass followed by lunch, 1.30 p.m. Rosary Procession, 2 p.m. Benediction and Exposition.

OUR LADY, HELP OF CHRISTIANS
CANUNGRA

There is no rose of such virtue as is the Rose that bore Jesu. Alleluia!

ANCIENT CAROL SUNG AT CANUNGRA

BERN AND MARGARET FOLEY, devout Catholics, moved in 1979 from Brisbane to Mount Tamborine, adjoining Canungra in the hinterland of Queensland. There was no priest there, but there was a chapel in the care of Father Ganzer, the parish priest of the nearby town of Beaudesert. Towards the end of the 1980s the Foleys went to see him and said that if they could have their own priest they would like to build a shrine to the Virgin.

The practical problems seemed insurmountable, but Bern and Margaret prayed for the help of St Joseph. Then one day Father Augustine Lazur and Brother Gabriel of the Order of St Paul the First Hermit arrived at Father Ganzer's house. Their shrine at Berrima was flourishing, and Augustine was looking for a place to build one in Queensland. Father Ganzer at once contacted the Foleys.

One of the ten chapels in the care of Father Ganzer was at Eagle Heights, Mount Tamborine, and next to it was a guest-house. The tenant wanted to retire and so, feeling that the house would be suitable for a chapel, shrine and monastery, Father Ganzer and the Foleys set about trying to raise the $55,000 needed to buy out the balance of the lease. After much prayer and many telephone calls, the money was raised and the project went ahead.

Father Augustine and Father Janusz came from Berrima and celebrated Mass in the newly founded monastery on the Feast of the Nativity of the Blessed Virgin, 8 September 1989. Soon afterwards, Father Janusz was appointed first rector of the monastery and shrine; the Foleys remained personally responsible for the lease. From that day onwards, Mass was said there daily.

❖ THE GIFT OF AN ICON

The custodians of the shrine wished above all to obtain an icon of the Black Madonna of Jasna Gora. To be authentic, it had to be made in Poland and would cost $1000. The icon was ordered in faith before the money was raised. When payment became due, a cheque for exactly that amount landed on the Foleys' doormat! Pilgrims soon began to arrive in large numbers, and on the Feast of Our Lady's Nativity they come in their thousands.

✤ A NEW SITE

A service in progress at the grotto at Canungra

The monks remained at Eagle Heights for seven years. The original location of the shrine was in a busy shopping centre, surrounded by private houses and traffic, so the custodians began to look for a new site. Augustine discovered an old dairy farm at Canungra. Peaceful, spacious and secluded, it was set on a little plateau surrounded by the cliffs of the Darlington range. After renovation and reconstruction, it was opened on 9 December 1995, the nearest Sunday to the Feast of the Immaculate Conception. The shrine is now cared for by three monks.

The 13th of each month is observed as Fatima Day. A grotto was built to house a wooden statue of Our Lady of Fatima, sent from Portugal. Great sheets of sailcloth are often used to cover the area where outdoor masses are celebrated.

Information for Visitors

Location: about 100 miles/80 km S of Brisbane on the Gold Coast and 8 km from Canungra on Beechmont Road. **Contact Number:** TEL AND FAX (7) 5533 3617.
Times of Services: weekdays 9 a.m., Saturday and Sunday 11 a.m., also 4 p.m. on Sunday. Fatima Day (13th of each month) 10 a.m. Exposition of the Blessed Sacrament, Adoration and Rosary, 11 a.m. Mass and Angelus, 12 noon lunch, 1 p.m. Eucharistic Procession to the Grotto, Benediction and Blessing of the Sick.

OUR LADY OF THE BOWED HEAD
VIENNA

'O Most Holy Virgin, most pure, nothing mortal is worthy to touch thy holy face, but since I have nothing to offer thee but my coarse handkerchief, do thou deign to accept it as a token of my goodwill.'

FRIAR DOMINIC OF JESUS AND MARY, BEFORE THE MIRACULOUS PICTURE, VIENNA, 1610

SOME MONASTIC Orders are enclosed, with strict rules of prayer and silence, and fasting at least one day a week. Others are what is known as 'discalced' – literally, 'without shoes'. Such an Order was that of the Austrian Carmelite Friars of the seventeenth century. These men spent their time wandering between religious houses, preaching and teaching as they went, taking their meals from local people. Dependent upon charity, they were known respectfully as 'mendicants' – a variety of holy beggars.

In 1610 Friar Dominic of Jesus and Mary was travelling the country in search of inexpensive houses which might provide lodgings for members of his Order. On this particular day, his task was the inspection of a run-down dwelling which the Carmelite Brothers had already purchased for that purpose. Rubbish had piled up outside and Dominic felt a strong urge to examine it for something valuable. But he dismissed his feeling; what could there be of interest or value in a pile of rubbish?

He went inside and began to inspect the rooms. But his curiosity returned, so he took his lantern back outside and poked about for a while. He was astonished when suddenly he came upon a painting of the Blessed Virgin. Dominic said a short prayer of apology to Our Lady for the way she had been treated, then took the picture back to his cell, cleaned it up and retouched the damage.

✤ I WILL ANSWER PRAYERS

Dominic venerated the picture daily, and one day the expression on the Virgin's face became animated. Dominic was terrified, thinking a trick was being played on him by the Devil. Then he heard the voice of the Virgin saying, 'Fear not, my son, for your request is granted.' He had not yet made any request, but the apparition continued: 'It will be accomplished, and it will be part of the reward in store for you in return for the love that you have shown for my Divine Son and myself.'

Dominic had earlier dreamt that the soul of one of his relatives was suffering in Purgatory. He knelt and prayed fervently for its deliverance. The Virgin assured him that this would be achieved if Dominic would offer several Masses for the soul's release. Later, Dominic received a vision in which Our Lady held the delivered soul in her hands. She told him that similar favours would be granted to those who honoured her through the miraculous picture.

To facilitate more widespread devotion to the picture, in accordance with Our Lady's wishes, Dominic arranged for it to be housed in the Oratory of St Charles near the Church of Santa Maria della Scala. Copies were also made of the picture, and soon there came reports of cures and favours received by those who had venerated it.

✤ A MUCH-TRAVELLED PICTURE

Dominic died in Vienna on 16 February 1630. After his death Duke Maximilian of Bavaria, a devout benefactor of the Carmelites, asked if he might borrow the picture. It was taken to his residence in Munich by Brother Anastasius, a Franciscan who had been a close friend and travelling companion of Dominic. Brother Anastasius signed a sworn testimony, dated 7 August 1631, to assure the authorities that everything he had heard from Dominic was true.

Duke Maximilian kept the picture for a while and daily said prayers before it. Then he gave it to the Carmelites in Munich, and they in turn handed it back to the Emperor Ferdinand II who had richly endowed the Carmelites in Prague and Vienna.

The picture seemed destined to be forever travelling. After the death of Ferdinand, his widow Eleanor entered the Convent of the Discalced Carmelite Nuns which she had earlier founded in Vienna. And when Eleanor herself died in 1655 the picture was given back to the Friars.

At the end of the nineteenth century, the Carmelite Friars built a new church on Vienna's Silbergasse, and in 1901 the miraculous picture was placed above the altar and dedicated to Our Lady of the Bowed Head. Here it remains to attract many thousands of pilgrims and visitors to the city.

On 29 January 1676 the cause of Dominic was examined by the Sacred Congregation which rules and arbitrates in matters of faith and doctrine and he was declared 'venerable' in 1907 by Pope Pius X.

One of the most splendid events of the year is held on 12 September when the Name of Mary is celebrated with a huge procession and special Masses.

Information for Visitors

Location: in Silbergasse, Central Vienna. Vienna is the capital of Austria and has good international road, rail and air links.
Contact Number: TEL (1) 320 3340. **Times of Services:** Saturdays 6 p.m.; Sundays 8.30 a.m.; 9.30 a.m.; 11 a.m.; 6 p.m.; 7 p.m.

THE VIRGIN OF THE POOR

BANNEUX

'Believe in me, and I will believe in you!'
OUR LADY TO MARIETTE BECO AT BANNEUX, 15 FEBRUARY 1933

BANNEUX IS AN unremarkable village on the edge of the Ardennes Mountains. In 1933 the Beco family were living there in a small house built by the father, Julien, an unemployed wiremaker. There were seven children and the family were poor, living mainly on produce from their little vegetable garden. They were nominally Catholic and not conspicuously devout.

Mariette was the oldest of the children, aged eleven. On the evening of 15 January she was looking after two of her brothers who were ill, and at the same time watching out for their father to return. She was nervous and did not like the long dark winter evenings.

As she peered through the curtains she suddenly became aware of a bright light hovering in the middle distance. After a few minutes the light formed itself into a human figure – 'a beautiful lady', as Mariette later reported. The woman was dressed in white and blue and was holding a rosary. Mariette looked again and then called to her mother, Louise, 'A beautiful lady in our garden is

smiling at me!' Her mother looked out but saw only a vague form. 'Perhaps it's the Virgin Mary!' she exclaimed, not unkindly.

✦ ALL IN A WINTER NIGHT

At school the next day Mariette told her story to her best friend, Joséphine Léonard, who only laughed. This upset Mariette, so Joséphine wondered whether there might be something in it after all. After school the two girls went to see the parish priest, Father Louis Jamin.

A great change now came over Mariette, who had previously been rather unruly, much given to playing truant and neglecting her lessons. She began to prepare her schoolwork thoroughly, and each morning went early to church to pray.

On 18 January, at seven in the evening, Mariette went out into the garden. Her father followed her. The girl knelt down and began to pray her rosary. Her father watched in amazement as she raised her arms as if greeting someone. Again, as she later swore on oath, Mariette saw the figure she had first seen from the upstairs window: 'She seemed to be standing on a platform of smoke.' Her father, who could see nothing, rode off on his bicycle and returned with his neighbour Michel Charlesèche and Michel's son, who was about the same age as Mariette.

When the three returned, Mariette was walking out of the garden and into the road. 'She is calling me,' she said.

✥ THE VIRGIN OF THE POOR

They watched as twice she fell to her knees on the frosty ground and prayed earnestly. When Mariette later described what had been happening that night, she said, 'The Lady called for me to follow her to the spring. She asked me to put my hand in the water and when I did so she said, "This spring is to be dedicated to me." '

Mariette then returned home, went to bed and fell asleep. Father Jamin was sent for, and asked Julien Beco what the strange affair was all about. Julien, a lapsed Catholic, was in a highly emotional state and told the priest that he was certain his daughter had received visions of the Blessed Virgin. He made an appointment at the confessional for the following day and expressed his desire to return to the Church.

The next day, the apparition came again to Mariette at seven in the evening. Others gathered in the garden as she asked of the vision, 'Who are you, *madame*?'

The Lady replied, 'I am the Virgin of the Poor.' Again she led Mariette to the icy spring and told her that in the future it would relieve the sick of all nations. The following day the Virgin appeared again and said that she desired a little chapel to be built in her honour at Banneux. When the vision had departed, Mariette fainted. The Virgin did not return for several weeks, and Mariette was teased and taunted for her credulity.

Then on 11 February Our Lady appeared again to Mariette and guided her to the spring. The Virgin said, 'I come to relieve suffering.' Later Mariette was interviewed by Father Jamin and said, 'It would be pleasing to the Lady for me to make my First Communion.'

On the 15th, accompanied by her mother, Mariette went out again into the garden with her rosary. At once the Virgin appeared and Mariette fell to her knees. She said, 'Holy Mother, Father Jamin asked me to ask you to give us a sign.' The Virgin replied cryptically, 'Believe in me, and I will believe in you!' And then she vanished from sight again, having enjoined Mariette to 'Pray very much'.

On 20 February the lady appeared again, and said gravely to Mariette, 'My dear child, pray very much... Au revoir.'

On 2 March, in the pouring rain, Mariette again went out into the garden at around seven in the evening. Those who had observed her throughout the apparitions remarked how, as the child's conversations with the Virgin proceeded, her speech became more rapid and her voice was raised in pitch. On this occasion the young vision-ary knew that this was her last vision, because the Virgin said, '*Adieu*.' Before this she told Mariette, 'I am the Mother of God.'

The story of the apparitions at Beauraing is

related below. Some people in Banneux suggested that Mariette had invented her account of her visions after hearing of those events, which took place only about fifty miles/80 km away.

❖ A MIRACULOUS HEALING

In January 1935 a commission was appointed, on the authority of Cardinal Van Roey, to study reports of visions in Banneux, Beauraing and elsewhere in Belgium, all of which had occurred within a very few years. Mariette was interrogated so often that she said, 'Had I known all that I was compelled to endure, I wouldn't have said a word about my visions. I might instead have built, all by myself, a small chapel in our garden.'

But the people of Banneux themselves built the chapel to the Virgin, and it was dedicated on the Feast of the Assumption in 1933. Even before the shrine was completed, pilgrims to Banneux made claims of supernatural cures. For instance, a Spaniard named Benito Pelegri Garcia had a very badly injured right arm. His wife heard the stories about Banneux and insisted that they walk there from Barcelona. Benito thrust his arm into the spring and felt it to be boiling hot. He exclaimed, 'I have come all the way from Spain. If you are indeed the Virgin of the Poor, then prove it to me!' He withdrew the drain-tube from his arm and the wound healed immediately in front of many witnesses.

Bishop Kerkhof wrote an account of Banneux in which he noted twenty miraculous cures occurring between 1933

and 1938. During the Second World War, Cardinal Van Roey issued an encyclical in which he declared that the events surrounding the apparitions were worthy of serious study. On 22 August 1949, the Bishop of Liège affirmed in a pastoral letter that the eight appearances made by Our Lady to Mariette were to be believed.

❖ VISITING THE SHRINE

Banneux is now one of the most visited shrines of Our Lady in northern Europe. The little chapel requested by her has been replicated more than a hundred times throughout the world, and though a pilgrim church was subsequently built, the original chapel remains.

The modern shrine is vast and imposing but never cold or impersonal. Two stone circles indicate the places where Mariette stopped and knelt before Our Lady. The connection between Lourdes (see p. 81) and Banneux was established in 1958, when a piece of the rock from Massabielle was mounted into the spring.

In St Joseph's Chapel behind the Beco house is a statue of St Joseph with the Christ Child. The square where the pilgrims gather, the Esplanade, whose main altar was consecrated in 1959, has the form of an aqueduct, symbolizing water as a source of life. It is also called the Altar of the Magnificat.

On the left of the Esplanade is the Chapel of the Message. In one corner is a carved candlestick, symbol of the light of peace which comes to pilgrims through Mary's intercession. There is a majestic statue of Our

Lord, and on its pedestal the Beatitudes are carved in Latin.

The sheer number of visitors made it necessary to build the Pilgrim's Church, completed in 1985 shortly before the visit of Pope John Paul II. Set into the wall by the entrance is a stone from St Peter's in Rome.

Other centres for prayer and worship are the Chapel of the Sick and St Michael's Chapel, where the Blessed Sacrament is in exposition every day. Facing this chapel is a belltower containing a bell presented by the late Chancellor of West Germany Konrad Adenauer. A small building called the Queen of Prophets' Chapel contains a statue of Our Lady of Rwanda; the cross was made in neighbouring Burundi.

But the *pièce de résistance* and spiritual centre of the shrine remains the Chapel of the Apparitions, marking the spot where Our Lady appeared eight times. A picture by Léon Jamin shows the Virgin's illuminated figure as seen by Mariette and in the middle of the chapel a white marble plaque recalls the place where she first saw Our Lady. Here a text declares: 'She wanted to open her Motherly Heart.' The Blessed Sacrament is always reserved in the Tabernacle.

The shrine at Banneux is almost a small town in itself. Besides the hospital for sick pilgrims and the old people's home, the Vierge des Pauvres, there is the Poverello, which contains twenty-five beds for those with little money who may stay here for two or three nights.

As for Mariette Beco, she never adopted a life of outward piety and resisted suggestions that she should enter a convent. In fact she married a café owner and suffered much unhappiness though she still strives to live according to the Gospel of Christ. It was the Banneux villagers themselves who murmured at the time of the apparitions that Mariette was not particularly educated, refined or pious – so why should the Mother of God choose to appear to her, of all people? Much the same had been said at Lourdes in the case of Bernadette Soubirous.

The opening day for pilgrimages is 1 May. The Assumption, 15 August, is the occasion for an international pilgrimage. There has been a recitation of the Rosary every evening since 1933 without fail.

Information for Visitors

Location: 10 miles/16 km SE of Liège. The shrine is to be found in the Rue de L'Esplanade. **Contact Numbers:** TEL (43) 60 02 22 FAX (43) 60 82 39; English secretariat (Mrs Maria Hare) TEL AND FAX 0181 861 1543. **Times of Services:** 1 May–31 October: Sundays and Bank Holidays 8.30 a.m., 11.30 a.m. and 4 p.m. (French), 10.30 a.m. (international), weekdays 8 a.m., 11.30 a.m. and 4 p.m. (French); 1 November–30 April: Sundays and Bank Holidays 8.30 a.m., 11.30 a.m. and 4 p.m. (French), weekdays 8 a.m. and 4 p.m. (French).

OUR LADY WITH THE GOLDEN HEART
BEAURAING

Do you love my Son? Do you love me? Then sacrifice yourself for me.
OUR LADY TO FERNANDE VOISIN, 3 JANUARY 1933

IN 1932 ALBERT VOISIN was a lively boy of eleven with a fifteen-year-old sister, Fernande. One November evening they called for their friends Andrée and Gilberte Degeimbre and made their way to the convent school in their small home town of Beauraing to collect another friend, Gilberte Voisin, at the end of the evening study.

As they waited at the school door Albert suddenly cried out, 'Look, the Virgin Mary is walking over the railway bridge!' He was a notorious prankster, so the girls took no notice. But Albert assured them he was not joking. When at last they turned to look, they saw a woman in white strolling through the air above the bridge and the convent garden. The children were afraid and hammered at the door.

Sister Valeria came to the door with Gilberte Voisin. Gilberte looked towards the bridge and she too saw the apparition, but the nun saw nothing and told the children to go home. When she reported the alleged vision to Mother Théophile, the Superior, she was scolded for her credulity. The frightened children ran home to their respective parents, who were deeply sceptical and sent them to bed in disgrace for lying.

❖ A SECOND APPARITION

The following day the children were at the convent school as usual to collect Gilberte Voisin when the apparition reappeared. Strangely, the youngsters were not frightened this time. Again they tried to convince Madame Germaine Degeimbre, but without success. She advised Hector Voisin that in future he should collect his daughter from school himself if the two families were not to be held up to ridicule all over the town.

The next evening, at about six o'clock, the Degeimbre children wanted to go to the convent again in the hope that the Virgin would appear. Their mother refused at first, but then she had second thoughts: what if someone was playing a practical joke on the children? She decided to accompany them and get to the bottom of the mystery. Other neighbours joined the group and they all set off for the convent.

The children ran ahead and the adults heard their cries of delight: 'She is here! She is here again!' This time the vision appeared on the walkway between the garden and the convent door. Later the children reported that the Virgin was standing three feet above the ground. She wore a white dress and her hands were clasped in a gesture of prayer. Then she opened her arms to welcome them before vanishing. The adults saw nothing.

Later that night, Germaine decided to conduct further investigations on her own. Convinced that the children were not telling lies, she felt someone must be deceiving them with reflections or mirrors. The children begged to be allowed to go with her, and, when they were about to leave the garden, they saw the Lady in the hawthorn. And when they reached the convent they fell to their knees and began reciting the *Ave Maria*. Germaine walked towards the spot on which their eyes were fixed, but Andrée Degeimbre warned her mother not to go further for fear of offending the Virgin. After a few moments the apparition vanished, and the distraught children cried. Germaine and the other adults then made a thorough search of the garden for the supposed trickster, but found no one.

In school the next day, Mother Théophile addressed all the children severely and said there was to be no talk of 'visions'. Meanwhile Madame Degeimbre and Madame Voisin had been to see the parish priest, Father Léon Lambert. The priest said that during Mass on 8 December he would pray for clarification: were the children being duped or was the Blessed Virgin truly visiting them?

✢ WE WILL BE GOOD!

The following evening Mother Théophile padlocked the garden gate and let dogs loose in the yard as a further disincentive to the curious. Undeterred, the children went along as usual, followed by a small group of interested adults. Again the Virgin appeared and the young visionaries fell to their knees. The girls were silent but Albert asked them, 'Is this the Blessed Virgin?' The Virgin nodded affirmatively, so he added, 'What is it you want with us?' Then the girls spoke in chorus, as if in answer to a voice which they alone had heard: 'Yes, we will always be good.' After this the vision disappeared.

On Sunday, 4 December the children went again to the convent school at about 6.30 in the evening. This time they took with them a little boy who had polio and a blind uncle of the Degeimbre girls. Again they asked the vision to declare unambiguously whether she was the Blessed Virgin or not. Later they reported that she had nodded her head. They then asked her to heal the two sick people they had brought with them. There was no apparent response.

They returned again on the 5th, and this time the accompanying group had grown into a crowd. Albert asked the Virgin for some sign to convince the adults that the vision was authentic. On the following day, 6 December, the Feast of St Nicholas, the Virgin appeared holding a rosary and the children at once began to recite it. The Virgin asked them to return on the Thursday, the Feast of the Immaculate Conception.

Word of the apparitions had spread throughout Belgium, and on the Thursday twelve thousand people turned up. This time the children went into an ecstatic trance during which they were subjected to investigation by doctors who were interested in abnormal psychological states. One Dr Lurquin lit a match and held it under Gilberte Voisin's hand. She uttered no cry of pain, and later examination revealed no burn mark. The doctor also nipped and pinched the children, but drew no response.

In the following days not every child saw or heard the same phenomena, and so discrepancies and confusion arose. As a result Mother Théophile suspected that the Devil was involved, so on Christmas Eve she fastened a medallion of St Benedict to the tree in the garden where the Lady had appeared. The apparitions briefly ceased.

✦ PRAY VERY MUCH!

They resumed again on 27 December, when the Virgin told the children, 'My last appearance will happen quite soon now.' On the 29th nine thousand pilgrims arrived in the hope of receiving a miraculous sign. That evening, Fernande Voisin claimed to have seen the Virgin reveal a golden heart radiating heavenly light.

She alone saw this phenomenon, which made the subsequent interrogations even more ill-tempered. The youngsters were constantly interviewed and cross-examined by doctors and officials until they were tired out.

The statue which marks the site of the apparition of the Virgin Mary in Beauraing

On 30 December, Fernande and Gilberte Voisin and Andrée Degeimbre claimed they had seen the luminous golden heart; but only

Fernande said she had heard the Lady say, 'Pray very much.'

On 3 January 1933, thirty-five thousand pilgrims made the journey to Beauraing. The children at once went into an ecstatic trance and began to pray the *Ave Maria* in unnaturally high-pitched tones. Each child received a private message from the Virgin; they were all deeply touched and wept openly – all except Fernande, to whom the Lady had not appeared that evening. She was heartbroken.

Fernande knelt by the gate and began praying the rosary desperately. At that moment there was a brilliant flash of lightning and a clap of thunder. It was apparent from the look on Fernande's face that she could see the Virgin once again. After this the visions ended.

✛ BLESSINGS AND CURES

Enthusiasm for the visionaries' story competed with a mood of scepticism, so that controversy raged throughout Belgium. In May 1933 the Bishop of Namur set up a committee to evaluate the visions.

Then came the first reports of cures and blessings. A young girl, Pauline Dereppe, was healed of a severe bone disease after praying at Beauraing. A middle-aged woman, Madame Van Laer, was cured of her tuberculosis. As the news spread, the number of pilgrims increased phenomenally: there were two and a half million in 1933 alone.

All the children survived into adulthood, married and raised children. Albert became a missionary schoolmaster in the Belgian Congo. It was not until 1949 that the findings of the committee of inquiry into the apparitions at Beauraing were made public. The Bishop declared, 'The Commission has thoroughly studied the events and we are convinced of the supernatural character of the visions.'

✛ VISITING THE SHRINE

At the north-west end of the church is the Garden of the Hawthorn, marking the place where Our Lady first appeared to the children. This is also the site of the Railway Bridge. A lovely statue of the Virgin in Carrara marble stands to greet you. Two miraculous cures were officially recorded here: those of Maria Van Laer and Madeleine Acar. Here too are the very paving stones where the visionaries fell to their knees. Under the podium is the Crypt of St John, which contains a beautiful statue of Our Lady as well as stations of the Cross by Max Van Der Linden.

Don't leave without visiting the Votive Chapel and the commemorative stone to the pilgrimage of Pope John Paul II on 18 May 1985. Proceed through the Chapel of the Blessed Sacrament, where Mass is celebrated daily, to the Monumental Arch under which is the Altar to the Queen of Heaven.

At the head of the nave is the Upper Church which is reached by a stairway (there is a ramp for wheelchairs). On the right is a silhouette entitled *The Mother of God*, traced by Maurice Rocher and realized in ceramics by Alice van der Gaast. Under the Upper Church you find the Rosary Church with the ceramics of the Mysteries of the Rosary by

Max Van Der Linden and also the metal stations of the Cross by the Swiss artist Willi Buck.

Between the shrine steps and the Town Hall is the Marian Museum, which displays souvenirs of the apparitions including clothing worn by the visionaries themselves. Each year tens of thousands visit the chapel built near the little convent school. Beauraing has become one of the best-loved of all the shrines of Our Lady.

On 21/22 August each year an international pilgrimage takes place and the anniversary of the apparition is celebrated on 29 November.

On a typical day's pilgrimage you can find time to pray where the apparitions were seen and attend an audio-visual programme in various languages concerning the events of 1932 and 1933. The ceremony of Stations of the Cross in held either in the crypt or in the wooded park.

The Beauraing cemetery contains the tombs of Andrée Degeimbre and Fernande Voisin.

Information for Visitors

Location: 50 miles/80 km SE of Brussels. The shrine is to be found in Rue de L' Aubépine. **Contact Numbers:** TEL (82) 71 21 18 FAX (82) 71 40 75. **Times of Services:** weekdays 10 a.m. and 11.15 a.m.; Sundays and Feast Days: Easter – 30 October 9 a.m., 12 noon and 3.45 p.m.; November – Palm Sunday 12 noon and 3.45 p.m., from 2.00 p.m.–5.00 p.m. Exposition of the Blessed Sacrament, 6.30 p.m. Daily Rosary. **Special dates:** 15 August Children's Homage to Mary, 21–22 August Candlelight Procession and International Pilgrimage, 1st Sunday in October Diocesan Gathering, 29 November Anniversary of the First Apparition, 1st Saturday each month Day of Recollection, 2nd and 3rd Sunday each month Pedestrian Pilgrimage, Saturday after Ascension Pilgrimage for Vocations.

— BOSNIA —

THE VIRGIN OF MEDJUGORJE

*The happenings in Medjugorje have done more for the world's faith than all the
pastoral work of the last fifty years.*

ARCHBISHOP FRANE FRANIC

THE NAME OF the village of Medjugorje means 'between the hills', which are called Crinca, Podbrdo and Krizevac. On the afternoon of 24 June 1981, fifteen-year-old Ivanka Ivankovic and her friend Mirjana Dragicevic, a year older, were walking from the next village, Bijakovic, towards Medjugorje. As Ivanka looked towards the summit of Podbrdo she suddenly exclaimed that she could see the Virgin Mary. Her companion dismissed the remark as meaningless. But when Mirjana looked she too saw something that resembled a human figure: it was white, and it was moving.

The two girls were afraid and ran to the nearby house of Marija and Milka Pavlovic. They told thirteen-year-old Milka what they had witnessed and, when the three of them went out again, they all saw the figure. Excitedly they ran into Medjugorje to find yet another friend, Vicka Ivankovic, who was sixteen. She was asleep, so the girls left a message that she was to meet them at the house of a boy named Jakov Colo, which had a good view of Podbrdo.

But when she arrived Vicka was too scared to look where they were pointing. Instead she dashed out of the house and gabbled her friends' extraordinary tale to two young villagers, sixteen-year-old Ivan Dragicevic and twenty-two-year-old Ivan Ivankovic. The young men were bolder and said they would accompany her to the top of Podbrdo. But as they climbed they all saw the figure and the younger Ivan ran back down again, terrified. Vicka stood her ground and began to make out the figure's dress and dark hair. The

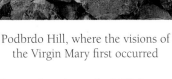

Podbrdo Hill, where the visions of
the Virgin Mary first occurred

apparition gestured to the young people to come closer, but they were too scared to do so.

Despite their fear they were also fascinated. So the following evening they returned and were rewarded with a vision. Later Vicka described the Madonna: 'She had curly black hair, blue eyes and rosy cheeks. She was still and very beautiful.' They all agreed that her dress was grey or light brown, and that she wore a veil.

Our Lady explained her presence on the hill: 'I have come to Medjugorje because I have found faithful people here. You must say seven times the Lord's Prayer, the Hail Mary, the Gloria and the Creed.'

By this time, as news of the young people's experience spread, there were adults at the bottom of the hill watching. But they were unable to see the Virgin.

❖ PEACE WRITTEN IN THE SKY

Next evening, with news of this second vision, huge crowds gathered. At six o'clock a mysterious light appeared above the hill. The young people ran towards it, crying out that the Virgin had returned. They sang psalms and said the Rosary.

Vicka, who was still afraid, had brought some holy water with her. She intended to sprinkle the vision with it – if it were the Devil, it should disappear. But the Virgin reassured Vicka: 'I am the Blessed Virgin Mary. Peace. Peace. Peace. Be reconciled.'

Next morning the children were summoned to the police station in the town of Citluk, where they were questioned and examined by a psychiatrist. The visions

continued, so the Communist authorities banned public meetings on Podbrdo.

The young people asked the Madonna if she would appear in church instead of on the hill, to which she agreed. After this, the visions sometimes appeared in people's houses too. In an attempt to control the ever-increasing crowds, the authorities closed off the hill with barricades. On 6 August, the Feast of the Transfiguration, some of those present said they had seen the word *Mir*, meaning peace, written in the sky.

❖ SECRETS CONCERNING THE END OF THE WORLD

On the 15th, the Assumption of the Blessed Virgin Mary, thousands crowded into the little village. The authorities, frustrated in their attempts to suppress these extraordinary events, arrested the parish priest on grounds of subversion. Father Zovko, who had come to believe in the apparition even though he had not personally seen it, was sentenced to three and a half years in prison.

The Bishop of Mostar, Pavo Zanic, tried to discipline the parish priests in the area for encouraging their flock to believe what he regarded as foolish stories, for contributing to disorder within the diocese and for compromising the reputation of the Catholic Church. When the young people pleaded with the Virgin to help the priests, she replied that the Bishop was wrong and should repent. On hearing of this exchange he was outraged, refusing to believe that the Mother of God would speak in such a way about someone in his position.

Meanwhile the visions continued daily in the church in Medjugorje, always urging peace and reconciliation and always in Croatian. In retrospect, given the appalling slaughter that was to take place in Bosnia, these messages seem like an awful warning. On 21 July the Virgin declared that fasting and prayer could prevent war and that God would be glorified in Russia. Church attendances rose spectacularly.

In 1982 the Virgin began to appear to the young people individually, and told them they would be given ten secrets about the end of the world. Mirjana was the first to receive all ten. Then the Virgin told her that she would only appear to the young girl on her birthday, 18 March. Mirjana was so distressed that the Virgin relented and began to appear to her on the second day of each month.

✤ Cures and blessings

The visions persist year after year and millions of pilgrims make the journey to Medjugorje, undeterred even during the bloody civil war following the breakdown of Communism. There are many reports of cures received and spiritual blessings given. Although the Bishop of Mostar never came to believe in the visions, the Archbishop of the adjacent diocese, Frane Franic, supported the young people's testimony and declared, 'The happenings in Medjugorje have done more for the world's faith than all the pastoral work of the last fifty years.'

In adulthood the young people retain their religious convictions and their faith in the visions. In 1990 the Convocation of Yugoslavian Bishops announced that they would continue their investigations and were not yet certain whether the visions were of supernatural origin.

The modern St James's Church is the centre of the Marian phenomenon which characterizes Medjugorje today. The place has been transformed into one of the most famous centres of devotion to the Virgin. Once a rural backwater, Medjugorje now boasts restaurants, shops and hotels.

Pope John Paul II encouraged pilgrims to go to Medjugorje before the outbreak of the civil war, and many thousands continued to visit the shrine throughout the troubles. Journalists, covering the war for their newspapers, often turned aside to examine the place where the Virgin appeared. A highlight of any visit is Friday's solemn procession to Podbrdo.

Information for Visitors

Location: between Dubrovnik and Mostar, in the remote mountains of southern Hercegovina. **Contact Numbers:** TEL (88) 651 011 FAX (88) 651 444. **Times of Services:** every hour every morning in the European languages; Monday–Saturday 10 a.m. in English, Sundays 11 a.m. in English, 5 p.m. (winter) and 6 p.m. (summer) Prayer of the Rosary, Wednesdays and Fridays solemn procession to Podbrdo.

CANADA

OUR LADY OF THE ROSARY
CAP DE LA MADELEINE

Do you see it? The statue has opened its eyes.
FATHER FRÉDÉRIC, 22 JUNE 1888

FRENCH CATHOLIC settlers began to arrive in large numbers in Canada in the early seventeenth century. They believed that they had enjoyed Our Lady's protection during the long sea voyage across the stormy Atlantic, so naturally they prayed for her help as they made their homes in a new land.

Three Rivers was a small trading port consecrated to the Immaculate Conception by the Society of Jesus in 1634. As trade increased, the original settlement divided and the newer part was named Cap de la Madeleine. The first parish priest, Father Jacques Buteux, was murdered in a raid by native Iroquois in 1652.

At about this time Pierre Boucher, Governor of Three Rivers, built a church and set up a little shrine to the Virgin, which in 1694 became the centre of a local branch of the Confraternity of the Holy Rosary. The population increased and a larger church was built in 1720, but the original wooden chapel was later commemorated by a small replica set up in 1940 and dedicated to Our Lady of Peace.

In 1855 an anonymous benefactor provided a huge statue of Our Lady in honour of the recent promulgation of the doctrine of the Immaculate Conception. This statue is now the centre of Cap de la Madeleine, the Church of Our Lady of the Cape, Queen of the Most Holy Rosary, Canada's national shrine. It is a figure of the Virgin standing barefoot, trampling the head of a snake in fulfilment of the Old Testament prophecy 'Thou shalt bruise the serpent's head' and of the promise that God will 'finally beat down Satan under our feet'.

✤ THE PIG AND THE ROSARY

But in the mid-nineteenth century there was apathy and slackness in Cap de la Madeleine. When Father Desilets went to church, on Ascension Day 1867, his congregation consisted of a solitary pig in the Lady Chapel, chewing a rosary! The priest subsequently preached vehemently on the subject of 'The Pig and the Rosary' to shame his parishioners, and very quickly the congregation increased.

An even larger church was now required, for which the stone had to be brought in winter from a quarry on the far side of the St Lawrence River. Normally this would have been easily accomplished by using sledges over the ice, but the winter of 1879 was mild and the river did not freeze. Building was brought to a standstill.

Father Desilets prayed to Our Lady for a bridge of ice. Although the winter was almost gone – it was mid-March – a tremendous storm blew packed ice from the banks into the middle of the river where it formed a bridge. In thanksgiving, Father Desilets preserved the old chapel by the side of the new church and designated the altar 'Our Lady of the Rosary'.

✣ THE STATUE OPENS HER EYES

The restored Lady Chapel was dedicated on 22 June 1888. That evening a lame man called Pierre Lacroix was brought into the chapel by Father Desilets and Father Frédéric. The three men experienced an amazing apparition centred on the statue of Our Lady. 'She raised her eyes!' Father Desilets later reported. 'She looked in front of her as if looking outwards into the distance. Her face was severe and rather sad.'

The three men swore an oath that what they had seen had truly taken place, and their statement is stored on parchment in the library of the sanctuary to this day. Pierre Lacroix's testimony reads:

I went into the shrine at about seven o'clock in the evening, accompanied by Vicar-General Luc Desilets and the Reverend Father Frédéric. I was walking between the two of them, helped by them. After praying for a while, I looked up at the statue of the Blessed Virgin which was facing directly towards me. As I did so, I saw most distinctly the statue with its eyes wide open in a most natural manner. It was as if it was looking out over our heads towards Three Rivers.

I examined this closely without saying anything. Then Vicar-General Desilets, leaving his place on my right, went across to Father Frédéric and I heard him say, 'Do you see it?'

'Yes,' said Father Frédéric, 'the statue has its eyes open, hasn't it? But can this really be true?'

I then told them that I had seen the same thing. And I make this solemn declaration believing it in conscience to be true and knowing that it has the same force and effect as if made upon oath.

Pierre Lacroix's testimony was counter-signed by Father Desilets.

After the miracle of the ice bridge and the apparition of the statue, pilgrims started to converge on Cap de la Madeleine from all over Canada. Their numbers increase year by year. Father Frédéric immediately began a mission to preach the name of the Blessed Virgin throughout the nation, and in 1902 he encouraged the diocesan bishop to install the Oblate Missionaries of Mary Immaculate to supervise the pilgrimages and to be stewards of the shrine.

❖ THE ONLY CROWNED MADONNA IN CANADA

The shrine of Our Lady at Cap de la Madeleine is one of the most beautiful of all the world's churches dedicated to the Blessed Virgin. It is set in magnificent gardens: the Garden of the Rosary and the Garden of the Stations of the Holy Cross. The bridge which connects the two is suspended on chains which represent the beads of the rosary. The final Station of the Cross is designed to resemble the Church of the Holy Sepulchre in Jerusalem. The statue's golden crown was a gift of the Franciscans in 1904, and the rosary which she is holding is made from wood from the olive trees in the Garden of Gethsemane. Some of these trees are at least two thousand years old and must therefore have been in Gethsemane on the night when Our Lord was betrayed and taken to be crucified.

Over the years Canada's national shrine has greatly expanded its missionary functions. The Cenacle of the Queen of the Apostles was opened there in 1937 as a retreat home visited by thousands of pilgrims every year. A journal, *Annals*, is devoted to homilies and meditations on the person of Our Lady and to publicizing the shrine. First published in 1892, it now has a circulation of more than seventy thousand. In recent times the shrine has been greatly extended and designated a basilica; it receives more than a million pilgrims annually. A novel way for visitors to arrive is by steamboat up the St Lawrence.

The statue of Our Lady of the Holy Rosary was crowned under the authority of Pope Pius X in 1904 and again under the authority of Pope Pius XII: it is the only crowned Madonna in Canada. Pope John Paul II made his personal pilgrimage on 10 September 1984.

In 1988, the centenary of the apparition, Father Frédéric, one of the first visionaries, was beatified. Many cures and accounts of spiritual blessings have been attested in the name of the Virgin who opened her eyes.

Information for Visitors

Location: at Three Rivers on St Lawrence Seaway 65 miles SW of Quebec and 75 miles NE of Montreal. **Contact Number:** TEL and FAX (819) 374 2441. **Times of Services:** April – October: 11 a.m., 4 p.m., 7.30 p.m., with a 2.30 p.m. service for coach parties. Winter services are held daily at 11 a.m. and 4 p.m.

— ENGLAND —

Our Lady of Caversham

BERKSHIRE

This morning the King rode forth very early to hunt and the Queen is ridden to
Our Lady of Caversham.

A NOTE IN THE JOURNAL OF ELIZABETH OF YORK (HENRY VII'S WIDOW) CONCERNING A
VISIT TO THE SHRINE BY CATHERINE OF ARAGON, 17 JULY 1532

IN THE THIRTEENTH CENTURY, the Benedictine monks of Reading decided to build a bridge across the Thames at Caversham where there was a little island. It seemed a perfect place in which to erect a chapel to St Anne, Mother of Our Lady, and they signified their intention to King Henry III. He approved and sent an oak tree from the Forest of Windsor to provide wood for the chapel roof.

Caversham had long been a centre of Marian devotion. Walter Gifford, Earl of Buckingham, founded an abbey at nearby Notley in 1162 and endowed St Peter's Church, Caversham in 1199. There was a Chapel of Our Lady nearby at this time.

Once the bridge had been built, the shrine of Our Lady of Caversham was transferred to the island and took its place next to the chapel of St Anne. The Benedictines were well connected and the shrine at Caversham was richly endowed. For example, in 1439 Countess Isabel of Warwick gave 'to Our Lady of Caversham, a crown of gold made from my chain and other gold in my cabinet to the weight of twenty pounds'. It was one of the richest crowns of Our Lady in Europe at that time and was regularly visited by the great and the good. Henry VIII himself made a pilgrimage to the shrine on 17 July 1532.

But at the time of Henry VIII's quarrel with Rome and the subsequent dissolution of the monasteries, the shrine at Caversham was looted by Thomas Cromwell on behalf of the King. Cromwell's infamous commissioner, Dr London, reported: 'I have pulled down the image of Your Lady at Caversham, with all its trinkets, shrouds, candles, wax images, crutches and brooches and I have thoroughly defaced the chapel. The image is altogether plated with silver. I have put her in a box, fast locked and nailed. By the next barge it shall be brought to my lord, with her coats, cap and hair and divers relics.' After this desecration, typical of what was happening nationwide, the shrine fell into disuse for centuries.

✧ AN IMAGE IN WHITE MARBLE

Only after the Catholic Emancipation Act of 1829 did plans emerge for the restoration of the shrine. Even so, it was not until 1896 that the first public Mass was celebrated in the village, and at that time there were no more than a dozen local Catholics.

As numbers of Catholics increased, in 1903 a new parish church of Our Lady and St Anne was built. The following year a tower with bells was added. The parish was fortunate in having a wealthy benefactress who provided vestments, an organ, a high altar in marble, the south aisle, its altar and an eighteenth-century white marble statue of the Blessed Virgin. A new priest, Father Michael Williams, arrived in the parish in 1920. A superb administrator, he extended the church building, improved the school and generally increased the reputation of Caversham throughout the country.

✧ A VERY FEMININE IMAGE

Devotion so increased in Caversham that a larger church was consecrated in 1954, a Marian Year (see p. 6). Its altar is constructed from the foundations of the original chapel on the island in the Thames. Every year Caversham attracted thousands of pilgrims, many of whom wrote to the parish priest offering their testimonies of cures and blessings received.

The new church already contained a chapel

A statue of Our Lady at Caversham

dedicated to St Anne, and it was decided to build a chapel to Our Lady. A medieval oak statue for this splendid chapel on the north side was provided by a Catholic antique dealer. A truly imposing figure, in the course of time it has suffered what is obviously malicious damage to Our Lady's breast. The statue is a very human and feminine representation of the Virgin as she suckles the Infant Jesus. Her hair falls over her shoulders and

The Virgin and Child with St Anne and John the Baptist, c 1499, Leonardo da Vinci

ST ANNE

The mother of the Virgin Mary, St Anne, is not mentioned in the Bible but first appears in a second-century document. Emperor Justinian built a church dedicated to her in Constantinople in the sixth century.

Pope Urban VI ordered her Feast Day, 26 July, to be especially celebrated in England in order to popularize the marriage of Richard II to Anne of Bohemia in the fourteenth century. St Anne is Patron Saint of Brittany.

THE BENEDICTINES

This Order of monks was founded upon the rule of St Benedict (480–550), who established monasteries at Subbiaco and Monte Cassino. By the ninth century, most monks and nuns in Europe considered themselves members of the Order or family of St Benedict. Through their careful copying and preserving of manuscripts, Benedictines became the custodians of classical learning through the Dark Ages after the break-up of the Roman Empire in the 5th century and the invasions of tribes from the east which followed. The nineteenth century saw a strong revival of the Benedictine Order, which included the founding of the monastery of St Vincent, Pennsylvania in 1846. The Rule of St Benedict is a prescribed way of life for the monastic community. It is administered by the Abbot and its principal duty is the worship of the Divine Office.

down to her waist. The design suggests that it is of northern European origin, probably from the region of Utrech in the Netherlands, and it is regarded as an artistic masterpiece as well as an object of spiritual devotion.

It is a source of delight to local people and pilgrims alike that so many of the stones from the original shrine have been incorporated into the building of the new one. So continuity is maintained between the historical devotion paid by kings and queens of England and the living faith of modern times.

Caversham is a small shrine and there are no large scale commemorative events, but Masses are said on all the Feasts of Our Lady and the parish priest is very glad to arrange services for pilgrims – either to be conducted by himself or pilgrims' own priest by arrangement.

Information for Visitors

Location: on northern outskirts of Reading, reached via A4074 or A4155. **Contact Number:** Tel 0118 947 1787. **Times of Services:** Saturday 5.30 p.m.; Sundays 10.30 a.m. and 6.30 p.m.; 9.15 a.m. and 7.30 p.m. on Mondays, Tuesdays and Wednesdays.

St Mary and St Egwin, Evesham
Hereford and Worcester

In the Abbey at Evesham were enshrined three or four images of Our Blessed Lady St Mary, having in her lap Our Saviour Jesus Christ in the form of a little babe; and these were set at every altar, and right well painted and fair arranged in gold and divers colours to which the people that beheld them showed great devotion.

From a medieval account of Evesham Abbey

Evesham is an ancient market town set in rich countryside on the banks of the River Avon, not far from Shakespeare's Stratford. Towards the end of the seventh century, Egwin was made Bishop of Worcester; he at once made enemies because of the ferocity with which he tried to suppress pagan practices in his diocese. To escape from his opponents, he took refuge in a hermitage. Word of his strictness, most probably highly exaggerated, reached Rome and Egwin was commanded to travel to the Holy City and give an account of himself.

He decided he would make the journey as a penitent, so he fixed chains to his legs and threw the key into the river. Tradition says that he celebrated Mass at St Peter's as soon as he arrived and then sat down to a fish dinner. Inside the fish was an exact replica of the key he had cast into the Avon. When the Pope heard about this miraculous event, he dismissed all the charges against Egwin who was allowed to return to England at once. He was further honoured when King Ethelred of Mercia gave him the land on which his hermitage had been built.

✧ Three miraculous women

Not long after Egwin's restoration, a swineherd named Eoves saw an apparition of three supernatural women singing psalms and heavenly melodies. He went for comfort and counsel to the saintly Bishop Egwin. Next day, Egwin himself went with his retinue to the same place, and saw the same vision. He looked at them steadfastly, particularly at the middle figure who was holding an open book and a golden cross. Egwin knew intuitively that she was the blessed Virgin. She made a sign of blessing with the cross and then her two maids disappeared.

Egwin promised to build a shrine to Our Lady on the site of his vision. He requested funds from King Ethelred, who generously provided land and money for a church.

In 704 the church was completed and staffed by Benedictines. Soon renowned throughout England, an abbey was also built there. It became a shrine to St Egwin and his bones were buried there.

After the Norman Conquest of 1066, an even larger church was erected – a great cathedral-like Gothic structure which took two centuries to build. Mass was said daily in honour of Our Lady, conducted on the grand scale with many priests and acolytes. There were written medieval records of a statue of the Madonna and Child, but no trace of this image remains after the savage destruction of the abbey at the dissolution of the religious houses in the sixteenth century.

However, after the Reformation the title of Abbot of Evesham was attached to the English Benedictines at Woolhampton in Berkshire. In this way, ancient connections have been maintained through the main shrine of Our Lady in Evesham.

❖ THE EVESHAM PRAYER CARDS

In 1889 the Passionist Fathers, founded by St Paul of the Cross in 1737 and named after their vow of devotion to the Passion of Our Lord Jesus Christ, arrived and built a little chapel in Evesham. Eleven years later the parish was given its own priest, Monsignor Patten, who built a new church named after the Immaculate Conception and St Egwin. Between the two world wars the parish priest, Father Arthur Proudman, published *The*

Evesham Prayer Card which is now widely used by pilgrims.

❖ THE SHRINE TODAY

Since the 1930s there has been an increasing flow of pilgrims and visitors to this ancient site. In 1952 there was a great procession when a new statue of the Blessed Virgin was carried from Our Lady's Church in Evesham High Street to the place where the ancient shrine stood by the river; this is now an annual event.

The big day of the year for Evesham is the annual pilgrimage which is always held on the second Sunday in June. People gather at the church for a picnic lunch and process through the town to the abbey park where Mass is celebrated at 3 p.m. Enriching the regular spiritual life of the shrine is a daily Rosary, said after the 10 a.m. Mass. There is also a Novena on Wednesdays at 7 p.m.

Information for Visitors

Location: on A44, close to junction 9 on M5. **Contact Number:** Tel (01386) 442 468. **Times of Services:** Sundays 8 a.m., 10 a.m. and 6.30 p.m.; Daily Mass 10 a.m.

THE BLESSED VIRGIN OF GLASTONBURY
SOMERSET

The plate of Glastonbury, golden to the weight of 11,000 ounces. Much furniture. In ready money more than £1,100. Many rich copes and other vestments. Debts owing to the Abbey of more than £2,200.

TREASURE LOOTED FROM GLASTONBURY ABBEY BY THE COMMISSIONERS FOR KING HENRY VIII, IN 1539

AN ANCIENT legend says that St Joseph of Arimathea, who begged Christ's body from the Roman Governor Pontius Pilate, came to Glastonbury in Somerset in AD 63 and planted his staff on Wearyall Hill, the site of a pagan temple. The staff budded and Joseph took this miracle as a sign that he should build there a church dedicated to the Blessed Virgin.

Whether the story is true or not, it tells us that there was a chapel to Our Lady in Glastonbury even before Saxon times. In the early centuries of Christianity, its adherents were persecuted by some of the Roman Emperors. Yet outposts of the faith endured, thanks to the courage and persistence of hermits who lived lives of solitary devotion in isolated regions such as the West Country.

In 433 St Patrick inaugurated monasteries, for by this time the Empire was officially Christian, following the conversion of the Emperor Constantine who was crowned at York in 313. It is said that St Patrick was buried in the original crypt of St Mary the Virgin at Glastonbury. St David visited Glastonbury and placed on the altar of the Virgin a sapphire which stayed in its place of honour until confiscated by Henry VIII at the dissolution of the monasteries.

In the tenth century St Dunstan established the Benedictines at Glastonbury and they prospered, though the original Chapel of Our Lady was destroyed by fire in 1184. However a new stone church was consecrated two years later. On the south door is carved a representation of Eve and the Fall of Man as related in Genesis 3; on the north side is the figure of the New Eve, the Blessed Virgin. There are also carvings of the Annunciation, the Visitation, the Nativity and the Magi.

❖ A CRUEL PERSECUTION

The earliest royal visitor to the new church was Edward I, who arrived with Queen Eleanor in Holy Week 1278 to hear Mass celebrated by the Archbishop of Canterbury. The Church of the Blessed Virgin remained

The imposing ruins of Glastonbury Abbey

one of Christendom's most famous shrines until the terrible desecration of 1539. On 19 September Henry's Commissioners dissolved the monastery. A huge quantity of treasure was removed and placed in the King's coffers in London. The Abbot, Richard Whiting, was hanged, disembowelled, beheaded and quartered.

✤ A BOUQUET OF ROSES

The true restoration of Glastonbury as a place of Christian pilgrimage did not take place until 1903 when some exiled French nuns, the Sisters of Charity at St Louis, were looking for a new convent in the West Country. They found a home at Minehead and also

THE DISSOLUTION OF THE MONASTERIES

In 1534 Henry VIII broke with Rome and proclaimed himself Supreme Head of the English Church. He had wanted to divorce his childless wife, Catherine of Aragon, and remarry in the hope of producing an heir, but the Pope had refused him. The vast wealth and property owned by the monasteries were also a great attraction, and in 1538–9, under Henry's minister Thomas Cromwell, the religious houses were destroyed and their property confiscated.

THE GLASTONBURY PRAYER

Lord, teach us to treasure all your words and ponder them in our heart. We ponder also the words you taught Mary to say and we make them our own. Lord, we glorify you. We rejoice in you, our Saviour. We thank you for the wonders you have worked for us. We praise your name, we trust in your loving mercy. Help us to do whatever you tell us. Bless the sick, the disabled and all in need. Our Lady of Glastonbury, pray for us.

rented a house by the ruined Abbey at Glastonbury. After years of poverty and hardship, the sisters were eventually able to purchase a fine house and gardens beside the stables which had formed their original dwelling near the holy site.

In 1940 the foundation stone for a new Church of the Blessed Virgin was laid and it was consecrated by the Bishop of Clifton the following year. Wartime restrictions determined that the church must be plain and functional, and the result is a building of pleasingly elegant simplicity. It was not until July 1955 that the present shrine of Our Lady was dedicated within the new Church of St Mary, beside the ruined Abbey.

The shrine was designed by the Bristol architect E. Whitmarsh-Everiss and the statue carved by P.L. Clark, who had been respon-

sible for the creation of some beautiful images of Our Lady which adorn many Catholic churches in London. Our Lady is crowned and holds the Infant Jesus on her arm. She also holds a bouquet of roses as the Christ Child raises his right hand in blessing. The tapestry either side of the statue was woven in 1965 and depicts saints with local connections.

✤ A SPIRITUAL CENTRE

Glastonbury, old and new, is a spiritual centre rivalled only by the Holy Land. Millions come each year to visit the ruined Abbey, and many pause to pray at the shrine of Our Lady at the end of Magdalen Street.

The July pilgrimage begins with a picnic lunch on the lower slopes of the Tor after which people process down the High Street to the Abbey for Solemn Concelebrated Mass at 3 p.m. Sick and lame people do not ascend the Tor but attend a service of prayer and healing in the parish church at 2.15 p.m. before going on to the Abbey Mass.

Information for Visitors

Location: on A39 between Bristol and Taunton. **Contact Number:** TEL (01458) 832 203. **Times of Services:** Sundays 8 a.m., 10.30 a.m. and 6.30 p.m. **Special Dates:** 1st Sunday in July Glastonbury Pilgrimage.

OUR LADY OF THE CRAG
KNARESBOROUGH, NORTH YORKSHIRE

In this place the Queen of Heaven did stretch forth her hand to save my son.
ATTRIBUTED TO JOHN THE MASON, C.1408

KNARESBOROUGH IS A beautiful market town on the banks of the River Nidd in the Yorkshire Dales. Its sturdy castle dates from 1070 and the town is also famous for Mother Shipton's Cave, the hermitage of the medieval prophetess who is said to have predicted motor cars, aeroplanes, space travel and the end of the world.

Steep cliffs rise from the river's edge and in one of these is the shrine of Our Lady of the Crag, a tiny cave measuring only about three metres high and two deep. Entry is by an arched wooden door, and immediately the visitor is impressed by an elaborate vaulted roof carved out of the rock. There are pillars and corbels, on one of which is carved a rose which predates the Tudor rose emblem first seen in the late fifteenth century. Opposite the arched entrance is a niche containing a statue of Our Lady.

Also carved by the entrance is the figure of one of the Knights Templar, a military religious order originally based in the Holy Land to protect pilgrims, who were then living locally at Little Ribston. He is undoubtedly portrayed as the guardian of the shrine.

The statue of the Madonna and Child, hewn in stone, dating back to the 1916 restoration

❖ THE POET LAUREATE AT KNARESBOROUGH

The shrine to Our Lady of the Crag was hewn out of the cliff-face in 1408 by John the Mason and is believed to be one of the oldest wayside shrines in Britain. John was a local stonemason who worked in a nearby quarry. His son was playing under the cliff one day when there was a sudden rock-fall, but he was unharmed even though he had been standing immediately under the rock-face when the boulders came crashing down. John attributed the boy's escape to the miraculous protection of the Blessed Virgin, and built the shrine in thanksgiving and as a perpetual commemoration.

The original wooden statue of Our Lady either rotted away over the centuries or was destroyed at the time of the Reformation. An elegant stone statue of the Madonna and

The exterior of the shrine showing the carving of the Knight Templar

Child now stands in the niche between two of the medieval pillars. This image was installed in 1916 when the shrine was bought and restored by John Martin, a Liverpool Catholic who then gave the shrine to Ampleforth Abbey on whose behalf it is now cared for by the Catholic parish of St Mary's, Knaresborough.

Protected by cliffs and set above the river among tall trees, the shrine of Our Lady of the Crag is a perfect haven for private prayer and quiet contemplation. Its many famous visitors have included the poet Wordsworth, who mistook it for the cell of the medieval hermit St Robert – an easy mistake, since St Robert's cave is set in the rock a mere three kilometres downstream.

The cave shrine is not large enough to allow Mass to be celebrated inside. Instead services are occasionally said in the open air on the hillside.

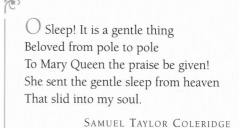

O Sleep! It is a gentle thing
Beloved from pole to pole
To Mary Queen the praise be given!
She sent the gentle sleep from heaven
That slid into my soul.

SAMUEL TAYLOR COLERIDGE
(1772–1834), 'THE RIME OF THE
ANCIENT MARINER'

Information for Visitors

Location: on A59 between York and Harrogate. **Contact Number:** TEL (01423) 862 388. **Times of Services:** by arrangement.

LADYEWELL
LANCASHIRE

So the drought shall yield the balm,
Dreams of beauty, pleasing calm.
So in grateful memory dwell
This tranquil spot, this hallowed well;
And may Our Lady's blessing be
Musing loiterer, e'er with thee.

EDWARD WILCOCK, 'THE LOITERER AT LADYEWELL', NINETEENTH CENTURY

AROUND 1100, AN IRISH merchant named Fergus Maguire was in danger of shipwreck in a severe gale off the Lancashire coast. His crew gave up and waited to die, but Fergus continued to man the helm while the storm raged, pouring rain and waves over him until he was almost drowned. His last hope disappeared when the wind tore the helm from his grasp. Fergus fell to his knees and prayed desperately: 'If Thou O Lord wilt save me, I will perform a holy act in honour of Thy name!'

The little ship was miraculously carried through the storm to the quiet waters of a secluded inlet. Fergus fell asleep after all his exertions and in a dream heard a voice saying, 'Go to Fernyhalgh, and there where thou shalt find a crab tree having coreless fruit hanging over a shrine, build me a chapel.'

❖ FERGUS AND THE CRAB APPLE BOUGH

In Liverpool Fergus asked to be directed to Fernyhalgh, but no one had heard of the place. Then he took a night's lodging in a village north-east of Liverpool where the lady of the house was chastising her maid for not returning sooner with the cows. 'But mistress,' pleaded the girl, 'it was the dun cow's fault for straying further than usual – as far as Fernyhalgh.'

Fergus leaped up and asked the maid to direct him there. He saw she was holding a branch of crab-apples, and when he examined them they were coreless. Next day she showed him where she had picked the branch, over a little well. Fergus was certain that this was the place he had dreamt of and immediately began to wonder how he might build a chapel there. As he walked up and down he noticed a stone which bore a worn image of a Madonna and Child. He realized that the place must be an old shrine to Our Lady that had fallen into disuse, and vowed to rebuild it.

The first mention of a shrine at Fernyhalgh is in the archives of the diocese of York, dated 8 January 1348. In 1547 the chapel there, along with many other churches and shrines, was destroyed and its wealth seized by King Edward VI. But with the accession of James II in 1685, persecution of Catholics eased and Ladyewell House was built as a Mass centre. On Our Lady's birthday in 1687, Bishop Leyburne confirmed 1099 men, women and children in the house. The chapel prospered over the years and became one of the best-known centres of Catholic faith and practice in the north of England. An eighteenth-century pastor who had received a large inheritance used it to build a seminary, Ushaw College.

Later a new Church of St Mary was built and Ladyewell House became a girls' school. In 1903 the Sisters of the Holy Child Jesus came to Ladyewell and Mass was said there again. The sisters renovated the ancient well and excavated the old stone steps, laid paving stones for the benefit of pilgrims and erected a statue of Our Lady of Lourdes which in 1935 was replaced by an image of the Madonna and Child.

Miraculous cures have been reported over the years. For example, in 1953 the Sisters avowed: 'We found a crutch by the well. It was left by a woman who claimed to be cured after praying a good part of the night there.' Before the Sisters left in 1985 Ladyewell was receiving as many as a thousand pilgrims a day.

❖ A BELL FROM ACROSS THE SEA

When the old Catholic diocese of Lancaster was restored Ladyewell became part of one of its parishes. In the Marian Year 1987 (see p. 6), the Bishop of Lancaster appointed Father Benedict Ruscillo and Catherine Stirzaker to be custodians of the shrine. A new road was built and a rose garden planted. The old altar from 1560 was preserved in an upper room which was made into a reliquary. An outside altar was erected, and in 1989 statues of St John Fisher and St Thomas More were set on the right and left of it.

In 1991 the beautiful Way of the Rosary was made, in which blue tiles from Portugal depict the fifteen mysteries. Later the outside altar was enclosed and became the Martyrs' Chapel which seats a hundred worshippers. A ship-shaped prayer room, named Stella Maris, was built by the well to recall the original witness of Fergus Maguire. In 1997 the Little Sisters of the Poor in Toulouse found on their property a bell engraved with a Madonna and Child and bearing the name Maguire. One of the Sisters had visited Ladyewell and heard the story of the twelfth-century merchant; it was conjectured that the bell had been the property of the Maguire family and taken by them to France during the persecutions of the sixteenth century. The bell was taken to Ladyewell that year. The most recent treasures

OPPOSITE The old well, renovated in 1903, and the statue of the Madonna and Child dating from 1935

to arrive at Ladyewell are the authenticated bones of St Thomas à Becket, who was martyred in Canterbury Cathedral on 30 December 1170. Its history, relics and facilities have made Ladyewell today a hugely popular pilgrimage centre, open daily.

There are many highlights in the year at Ladyewell including the celebration of Divine Mercy Day on the Sunday after Easter and the Day of Reparation on the nearest Saturday to 13 July. A moveable feast is the Lancaster Diocesan Pilgrimage. The Feast Day of Our Lady of Guadalupe is held on 12 December. Great spring and autumn occasions include the ceremonies of the Fifteen Mysteries of the Rosary, the Crowning of Our Lady and Benediction on first Saturdays in May and October.

Information for Visitors

Location: Fernyhalgh is near Preston, close to junction 32 of M6. **Contact Number:** TEL (01772) 700181. **Times of Services:** These vary to accommodate pilgrims' coaches coming from a distance. You can telephone to arrange to have Mass said at a time to suit your group. On days when no special arrangements are made, times are usually Sunday 11 a.m., Thursday and Friday 12 noon and Saturday 11 a.m., but visitors are urged to confirm these times beforehand. **Special Dates:** Main celebrations are Divine Mercy Day on Low Sunday, Day of Reparation on nearest Saturday to 13 July, Lancaster Diocesan Pilgrimage (date always to be fixed), Feast Day of Our Lady of Guadalupe on 12 December, Advent and Christmas Celebration on Saturday before Christmas Eve, Rosary Procession, Fifteen Mysteries of the Rosary, Crowning of Our Lady and Benediction on 1st Saturday in May and October.

LITTLE NAZARETH
WALSINGHAM, NORFOLK

*Walsingham is one of the few places in England where religious truth is not a matter of
external propositions but can be experienced in the heart.*

CANON CHRISTOPHER COLVIN, SOMETIME ADMINISTRATOR OF THE ANGLICAN SHRINE

HIDDEN AMONG gentle slopes in the soft
light of East Anglia lies the ancient
village of Walsingham, where there is not one
shrine to the Blessed Virgin but two. In the
Middle Ages Walsingham was known
throughout Europe as 'Little Nazareth'.

✦ THE WORK OF ANGELS

In 1061 Richeldis de Faverches, Lady of the
Manor of Walsingham, was
saying her prayers when she
received a vision of the Virgin
Mary. This was followed by a
twice-repeated vision of the
house of Joseph, Mary and the
boy Jesus at Nazareth, during
which Richeldis was
commanded to build a replica of
the Holy House – in which the
Annunciation took place – on
her own land for the use of
Crusaders as a focus of devotion. Richeldis gave instructions
for building to commence but,
according to legend, the

The Madonna and Child
(from the Catholic shrine)

following night she was awakened by the
sound of singing and when she went to
investigate she saw angels leaving. The Holy
House had been miraculously built, and very
soon pilgrims began to arrive.

Augustinian canons and Franciscan friars
had established houses here by 1130 and
catered for the needs of the many visitors,
both commoners and royalty: the shrine
received royal patronage from Henry III in
1226. All along the road to
Walsingham were built chapels
and refreshment houses, the
last of which erected in the
fourteenth century and
dedicated to St Catherine of
Alexandria, patron saint of
all Holy Land pilgrims, was
known as the Slipper Chapel.
Here pilgrims, out of respect,
would take off their boots and
approach the shrine either in
slippers or barefoot. The path
which leads from the Slipper
Chapel to the shrine is
currently being remade as part

of the Sacred Land Project (a project by all the major religious and environmental groups in Britain to revive and celebrate the sacred meaning and significance of sites).

✦ CHANGING FORTUNES

In the sixteenth century, the Protestant Reformation swept across northern Europe and resulted in widespread iconoclasm. In 1538 the shrine at Walsingham was destroyed and its statue of the Virgin transported to London and burnt. Subsequently the Slipper Chapel was used as a poor house, a forge, a cowshed and a barn.

Under the Catholic Emancipation Act of 1829, freedom of worship was restored. The Anglican Church too enjoyed a revival through the Oxford Movement, whose leaders such as Newman (later Cardinal), Keble and Pusey venerated the ancient forms and traditions of the Catholic faith. In the Sussex village of Buxted supporters of the Movement built a new church with a Lady Chapel to the exact dimensions of Lady Richeldis's original. Alfred Hope Patten, a local boy, prayed regularly at Buxted and in due course was ordained in the Church of England. In 1921 he was appointed to the living of Walsingham where he remained for the rest of his life.

Patten supervised the carving of a stone statue of the Madonna and Child based on the model of the original Walsingham Abbey Seal which is preserved in the British Museum. Since 1922 prayers and Rosary have been said before the statue each night in unbroken succession. Using medieval references, in 1931 Patten re-created Lady Richeldis' Holy House in brick and stone, and seven years later the present Pilgrimage Church was built to cover and protect it. The

---

THE AUGUSTINIANS AND THE FRANCISCANS

The Augustinians, also known as the Black Canons, are communities of monks who originally banded together in the eleventh century in northern Italy and southern France to live in poverty, chastity and obedience. They followed the practical and adaptable Rule of Augustine and were involved in pastoral work. In London, St Thomas's and St Bartholomew's hospitals were originally Augustinian houses.

The Franciscans or Friars Minor, preachers and missionaries, were founded by St Francis of Assisi in 1209. Their rule insists on complete poverty, and the Friars were instructed to live by the labour of their hands or by begging. They were not allowed to own property. In the fourteenth century a compromise allowed communities as a whole to own their monastic house.

The Madonna and Child (from the Catholic shrine)

cloister houses an Anglo-Saxon well. This is a beautiful place which resonates with spiritual calm and a palpable silence.

❖ TWO SHRINES, ONE FAITH

While the Oxford Movement revived devotion to the Virgin in the Church of England, Roman Catholics were enjoying freedom of expression for the first time since the Reformation. In 1863 Charlotte Pearson Boyd purchased the old Slipper Chapel and in the following year Pope Leo XIII gave permission for the restoration of the original Catholic shrine. On 20 August 1897 the first public pilgrimage here from Kings Lynn took place. So by the end of the nineteenth century the little Norfolk village was home to two flourishing shrines of Our Lady.

On 19 August 1934 Cardinal Bourne led the Catholic bishops of England and Wales and ten thousand pilgrims to the Slipper Chapel, and from this date it became the official Roman Catholic National Shrine. The four hundredth anniversary of the shrine's destruction was commemorated in 1938 by a Pilgrimage of Catholic Youth, and in 1948 fourteen oak crosses were set up in the garden. There is a tradition for pilgrims to walk the last mile here barefoot.

The Slipper Chapel contains a magnificent stone statue of the Virgin carved by Marcel Barbeau and crowned by the Papal Representative, Archbishop O'Hara, on the Feast of the Assumption in 1954. The statue was taken to Wembley to be blessed by Pope John Paul II when he visited England in 1982.

The clean, simple lines of the cloister

O England great cause have you to be
    glad
Compared to the Promised Land.
For you are graced to stand in that degree,
Through this glorious Lady's intercession;
To be called in every realm and region
The Holy Land, Our Lady's Dowry.
Thus you are called from all antiquity.
And this is the cause as appears by
    comparison:
In you is built New Nazareth, a house
To the honour of the Heavenly Empress
And of her glorious salutation,
First principle and ground of our salvation,
When Gabriel said at Old Nazareth, 'Ave!'
This joy shall be remembered here each
    day.

ANON, 'THE BALLAD OF WALSINGHAM', C.
1490, KNOWN AS 'THE PYNSON BALLAD'
AFTER ITS FIRST PRINTER

surrounding the Slipper Chapel provide a serene atmosphere. Here you will find the Holy Water Fountain and the baptismal font from the disused church of Forncett St Mary near Norwich.

The Churches responsible for the shrines at Walsingham are aware that the very fact of the existence of two shrines is a sign of disunity. In mitigation it should be said that the Anglican and Catholic shrines were restored before the ecumenical movement was established. Nowadays there is less competition than cooperation between the custodians of these spiritual resources. In particular, the

Our Lady of Walsingham (from the Anglican shrine)

Chapel of Reconciliation on the main Slipper Chapel site was blessed by Cardinal Hume in 1981; it contains the Icon of the Mother of God, painted for the Golden Jubilee in 1988 by Archimandrite David of the Russian Orthodox community of St Seraphim at Walsingham. The Chapel of Reconciliation can hold a congregation of six hundred, and upstairs in the Anglican shrine there is an Orthodox Chapel.

There are frequent pilgrimages throughout the summer months when there is a huge variety of activities and presentations available to visitors. A particular attraction is the Candlelight Procession of Our Lady on Saturday evenings at the Anglican shrine. A highlight at the Catholic shrine is the daily (Easter to October) Pilgrim Service at the church of the Annunciation or in Elmham House gardens at 8 p.m.

Information for Visitors

Location: on B1105 between Wells-next-the-Sea and Fakenham. **Contact Numbers for Catholic Shrine:** TEL (01328) 820217 FAX (01328) 821087. **Times of Catholic Services:** Easter to October (daily unless otherwise stated) 8.30 a.m. Angelus and Morning Prayer, 10.00 a.m. Procession, 11.00 a.m. Sacrament of Penance/Stations of the Cross in Chapel of Reconciliation, 12 noon. Angelus and Pilgrim Mass in Chapel of Reconciliation, 2.30 p.m. Rosary in Slipper Chapel, 3 p.m. Adoration of the Blessed Sacrament, 4 p.m. Evening Prayer and Benediction in Chapel of Reconciliation, 8 p.m. Pilgrim Service at Church of the Annunciation or in Elmham House gardens. Weekends follow the same programme until 2 p.m. Adoration of the Blessed Sacrament, 3 p.m. Benediction in Chapel of Reconciliation, 5 p.m. (Sundays only). Pilgrim Mass in Chapel of Reconciliation, 6 p.m. Evening Prayer in Church of the Annunication, 8 p.m. (Saturdays only). Pilgrim Service in Church of the Annunication.

Contact Number for Anglican Shrine: TEL (01328) 820255. **Times of Anglican Services:** daily 7.30 a.m. Easter to end October in the shrine, 11.30 a.m. in All Souls' Chapel in grounds. Other Masses listed on daily timetable in north aisle. Shrine Prayers, including intercessions asked for by pilgrims and visitors, are offered at 6 p.m. in the Holy House. Also 2.30 p.m. daily Easter to end October. Sprinkling at the Well. Weekends 6 p.m. Saturday Sung Mass, 8.15 p.m. Saturday Candlelight Procession of Our Lady, 2.30 p.m. Sunday Sprinkling at the Well, 4 p.m. Sunday Procession of the Blessed Sacrament.

—— FRANCE ——

THE THREE SHRINES OF CHARTRES

Arise, shine for thy light is come, and the glory of the Lord is risen upon thee.

ISAIAH 40:1

CHARTRES CATHEDRAL is renowned the world over for the magnificence of its stained glass windows. Friedrich Meyer, a nineteenth century Austrian historian and art critic, described the exquisite light which filters through them as 'the quintessence of luminescence'. A recurring motif in the glass is the life of Our Lady, to whom the cathedral is dedicated. Over the centuries three shrines of the Blessed Virgin have adorned this splendid building.

✦ DRUIDS AND KINGS

The shrine of Notre Dame de Sous-Terre is probably the oldest shrine to Our Lady anywhere in the world, built on the site of a pagan temple from before the birth of Christ. The Druids worshipped here and it is said that their shrine was dedicated to Matri Futurae Dei Nascituri – to the Mother of God as yet unborn. This tradition is supported by the discovery of druidic artefacts and religious emblems during restoration after the ravages of the Second World War.

The first Christian church on the site was made of wood, replaced in 1020 by a stone edifice – though the original crypt and underground grotto were preserved. In the early Middle Ages the shrine was attended by most of the Carolingian kings, and every French king except Louis XV and Louis XVI prayed to the Virgin at Chartres. There are records of pilgrimages by several English monarchs: Matilda, Canute, Richard I and Edward III.

Notre Dame de Sous-Terre once held a very ancient statue of Our Lady, famously described by the celebrated art historian Pintard in 1681:

The Virgin sits on a chair, her Son sits on her knees and he gives the sign of blessing with his right hand. In his left hand he holds an orb. He is bare-headed and his hair is quite short. He wears a close-fitting robe girdled with a belt. His face, hands and feet are bare and they are of a shining grey-ebony colour.

The Virgin is dressed in an antique

The carved statue of Our Lady
of Notre Dame de Sous-Terre

mantle in the shape of a chasuble. Her face
is oval, of perfect construction, and of the
same shining black colour. Her crown is
very plain, only the top being decorated
with flowers and small leaves. Her chair is
one foot wide with four parts hallowed out
at the back and carved. The statue is
twenty-nine inches tall.

During the Reign of Terror which
followed the French Revolution of 1789 the
statue was desecrated and then burnt. It was
not until the mid-nineteenth century that a

RIGHT Notre Dame de la Belle-Verrière, one of the
famous stained-glass windows from Chartres
Cathedral

replacement was provided, designed and
carved by the Paris sculptor Fontenelle.

❖ OUR LADY'S VEIL

The first church at Chartres boasted one of
the most venerated relics in Christendom,
Our Lady's Veil, which tradition declares was
worn by the Virgin as she stood by the Cross
on the first Good Friday. It had been transferred in the early years of the Christian
Church from Jerusalem to Constantinople
and presented by the Empress Irene to the
Holy Roman Emperor Charlemagne
(742–814). In 876 his descendant Charles

the Bald gave the relic to the cathedral at Chartres. Our Lady's Veil is kept in a golden reliquary beside the high altar and has formed the focus of many traditions throughout the centuries. For instance, in 911 when the bandit Rollo and his henchmen were besieging Chartres, local people took the veil from the church and paraded it as a flag of war. Rollo and his men were defeated and the siege was lifted.

The veil itself is more than six metres long and made of silk. If indeed it was the original Veil of Our Lady, it has obviously been much extended and embellished over the centuries. Every year on the Feast of the Assumption, 15 August, the veil is processed through the town.

The shrine is also renowned for pilgrimages made by many of the great doctors and theologians of the church including St Anselm (1033–1109), who devised a proof of the existence of God which is still regarded as cogent and valid by some twentieth-century philosophers.

✦ THE TOWER OF WAX

The third shrine in Chartres Cathedral is Our Lady of the Pillow or Notre Dame du Pitier, in the north aisle of the chancel. In the sixteenth century this statue was housed in a room above the rood, a screen featuring a cross at the junction of chancel and nave. There a huge candle was kept burning before it – the so-called 'Tower of Wax' – with the result that the wood darkened and the statue became known also as the Black Virgin. In 1763 the room over the rood was dismantled

and the statue removed to a marble pillar close by, which in 1806 was itself replaced by a column from the rood-loft.

The golden-haired Virgin sits on a throne, holding the Christ child on her knee and a pear. The Infant Jesus raises his right hand in a sign of blessing while in his left he holds a globe. The figure of the Black Virgin was crowned by Pope Pius IX in 1855.

The best time to visit Chartres, a place of pilgrimage for more than 1000 years, is on a sunny day when the light shows the windows to their best effect. There are more than 5000 figures in the stained glass, representing scenes from the Bible and the lives of the Saints.

Information for Visitors

Location: 60 miles/95 km SW of Paris.
Contact Numbers: TEL 37 21 75 02 FAX 37 36 51 43. **Times of Services:** weekdays 9 a.m., 11.45 a.m. and 6 p.m., Sundays 9.30 a.m., 11 a.m. and 6 p.m. The cathedral is open weekdays 7.30 a.m.–7.15 p.m., Sundays and Holy Days 8.30 a.m.–7.15 p.m.
Special Events: 15 August procession of Our Lady's Veil through Chartres, 8 September (the Virgin's birthday) and 8 December (Feast of the Immaculate Conception) commemoration of the Virgin, 15 September solemn procession around the crypt.

OUR LADY OF LA SALETTE

The story of the vision of La Salette bears in itself every mark of the truth and the faithful have grounds for believing it to be beyond doubt and certain.

BISHOP DE BRUILLARD, ADVENT 1851

ON THE MORNING of 19 September 1846 Maximin Giraud, aged eleven, and Mélanie Mathieu, fourteen, were leading a few cows up to pasture on a plateau in the foothills of the French Alps. Maximin was not a happy boy: his father drank heavily and his stepmother showed him little affection. Mélanie came from a very poor family who had sent her to work as a hired cow girl at the age of eight.

✦ A SPHERE OF BRIGHT LIGHT

At noon they heard the Angelus bells ring out from the church far below them in the village of La Salette. They were not devout, and the bells were a signal to stop for lunch rather than to pray. After they had eaten both children fell asleep, and when they awoke they had to go in search of the cows which had wandered away.

They found the animals near the edge of a ravine; when Mélanie looked down into it she was terrified and screamed, for she saw a huge, luminous globe. Maximin saw it too, and taking his herdsman's staff threatened to

hit the globe to drive it away. The children stood and gazed at the phenomenon with a mixture of terror and curiosity. As they did so, the sphere of light grew brighter and enlarged. Then it opened, as if a curtain of light was being drawn aside. Inside the sphere sat a woman, her head in her hands, weeping. Within a few minutes the globe had faded away, but the woman remained. She stood up and took her hands away from her face. 'How beautiful she is!' exclaimed Mélanie to Maximin. The lovely woman continued to weep and folded her arms across her breast. She wore a crown, a long white dress ornamented with roses, a shawl and round her neck was a necklace in the form of a Cross.

✦ DISOBEDIENCE AND BLASPHEMY

'Children, come to me!' commanded the apparition. She told them not to be afraid and added that she had important news for them. As the children drew nearer to the apparition, the luminous sphere returned and enclosed all three of them. The woman explained that her

Son was angry because of the disobedience of the local people: in particular, villagers were not keeping the Sabbath and the men blasphemed the name of Christ. Because of this wrongdoing the crops would fail and many children would die of disease. Then the apparition spoke to Maximin and Mélanie individually. They later reported that, as she did so, the one to whom she was not speaking directly could hear nothing.

She asked them if they said their prayers. Shamefacedly, the children confessed that they prayed hardly at all. The vision replied, 'It is most important that you pray each morning and evening. An Our Father and a Hail Mary – more if you have time.' The woman then complained that only a few old women attended Mass regularly and that nearly all the local people continued to eat meat throughout Lent. She also gave Maximin a sign to convince him that she was real and that he really was seeing her: 'Do you remember when once you were with your father and you saw some rotting wheat?' She reported precisely the conversation that had passed between the boy and his father.

The basilica at La Salette

The statue of Mélanie Mathieu marking the site of the original visions

Finally she told the children to report everything she had said to the people in their village Ablandins. Then she moved away to the far side of the ravine and rose into the sky, her face now joyful and transfigured. The sphere of light encompassed her again and she vanished.

❖ SOLEMN WARNINGS

When their employer, Pierre Selme, complained that the children were late in returning, Maximin told him about their vision. Selme just laughed. He knew that Maximin was a practical joker.

Later the children went to the home of Baptiste Pra, who owned some of the cows, and Maximin told his story again. Pra's mother questioned Mélanie, who corroborated Maximin's account to the letter and convinced the old woman. Fearfully she turned to her son: 'You have heard what the Virgin has said to the children. Are you still intending to go to work tomorrow – Sunday – after that?'

Baptiste was sceptical: 'The Virgin wouldn't appear to children like those two – children who don't even say their prayers.'

Selme announced that next morning he would make the children repeat their story to the parish priest, Father Jacques Perrin, who accepted their account at once. He used the Virgin's warnings as the basis for his sermon.

News of the vision spread rapidly around the neighbouring villages and the children were constantly being asked to repeat their story. A local councillor offered Mélanie thirty francs (recalling the thirty pieces of silver paid to Judas Iscariot for his betrayal of Christ) to say she had been mistaken, perhaps dreaming – the children had admitted that they had taken a long nap on the hillside. Mélanie threw the official's money back at him.

Then a new parish priest arrived to take charge of all the little villages for which the central church was La Salette. Father Melin recorded conversions to the active faith, increased confessions and better attendances at Mass.

A most moving conversation took place between Maximin and his father. Monsieur Giraud, half drunk, had cursed his son for making up the whole wild tale. But Maximin said, 'No, Father. The Lady spoke to me about you as well.'

Giraud replied, 'Me? What could she possibly have to say about me?'

Maximin repeated the conversation about the wheat, and Giraud was touched to the heart. When his wife made the journey to the place of the children's vision, he went with her. After this pilgrimage, he found that his asthma was cured. He stopped drinking and returned to the Church.

✤ MIRACLE CURES

A year later, on 19 September 1847, over fifty thousand people went to the place of the apparition and Masses were said. A dried-up spring there burst into life again. Two dozen cures of physical illness were reported to the parish priest and Bishop de Bruillard, diocesan for Grenoble, set up a committee of inquiry into the visionary experience.

Maximin and Mélanie, wearied by the constant procession of interrogators and miracle-seekers, were taken into the nearby convent at Corps and given formal religious education. Four years after the vision Maximin was taken to be interviewed by the famous Curé d'Ars, who carried the stigmata in his palms and was regarded by many as a saint. The Curé did not believe the boy's story. Eight years passed and the fame of La Salette increased. The Curé began to have second thoughts and asked the Virgin to inform him whether the boy had been speaking the truth. He received a miraculous sign, and from that day supported the vision of the Lady of La Salette.

✤ THE FATE OF THE VISIONARIES

Maximin proceeded to the seminary at Grenoble, while Mélanie was admitted to the convent of the Sisters of Providence at Corenc. They were required by Rome to write down all that the Lady had told them.

This is the month, and this the happy
  morn,
Wherein the Son of heaven's eternal king
Of wedded maid and virgin mother born
Our great redemption from above did bring.
For so the holy sages once did sing
That he our deadly forfeit should release,
And with His father work us a perpetual
  peace.

But see the Virgin blest
Hath laid her babe to rest,
Time is our tedious song should here have
  ending.

JOHN MILTON (1608–74),
'ON THE MORNING OF CHRIST'S NATIVITY'

Pope Pius IX was, by all accounts, delighted by Maximin's words, but disturbed by the dire warnings which the Virgin had issued to Mélanie.

Maximin did not have a true vocation and found theological studies irksome. He was apprenticed to a pharmacist for a time before becoming a mechanic, but even this practical trade did not suit him and he became something of a drifter. For a time he was a member of the Pope's bodyguard. Like his father he suffered from asthma, and he died on 1 March 1875, aged only forty.

Mélanie did not settle to convent life in France, where she was forever being pestered by visitors. For a time she lived with the Carmelite nuns in Darlington in the north of England, but she did not take to the silent, contemplative life. Finally the Bishop of Altamura in Italy, seeing how troubled and rootless Mélanie was, provided her with a room in his palace. She lived out her days there, quietly and devoutly, and died on 15 December 1904, aged seventy-three.

✤ A PLACE OF PEACE AND BEAUTY

A magnificent basilica, built in 1879, is now set in the spectacular mountain scenery and the whole location is a tremendous encouragement to prayer and contemplation. The atmosphere is of sustained peace and beauty. The shrine welcomes pilgrims all year round, except November.

Don't miss the statues which mark the places of the original apparitions and the spring which flowed after Our Lady's visitation. The shrine offers audio-visual presentations and there is a retreat centre.

The summer months are busiest and pilgrims should book in advance, while the alpine winter provides exactly the right atmosphere for silent meditation.

The Feast Day of Our Lady of Salette is celebrated on 19 September when many thousands of pilgrims attend the shrine.

The shrine is some 2000 metres in the Alpine foothills, but is easily accessible by public and private transport.

Information for Visitors

Location: 50 miles/80 km S of Grenoble, near village of Corps on N85. **Contact Numbers:** TEL 76 30 00 11 FAX 76 30 03 65. **Times of Services:** weekdays 10.45 a.m., Sundays 10.15 a.m., 11.30 a.m. and 4 p.m.

OUR LADY OF THE SMILE
LISIEUX

O Mary, Mother of Jesus and our Mother too, who once by a visible smile didst graciously console and cure thy privileged child Saint Thérèse of the Child Jesus, we beseech thee, come to us also to console us in the troubles of this life.

FROM THE CARMELITE PRAYER TO OUR LADY OF THE SMILE

MOST OF THE great saints and visionaries do not leave autobiographical writings. We are fortunate indeed that the superiors of St Thérèse of Lisieux (1873–97) commanded her to write her life story, *L'Histoire d'une Ame* (usually translated *The Story of a Soul*), published posthumously in 1898. It is one of the classic texts of spirituality, remarkable for its plainness and simplicity.

Thérèse was born at Alençon in 1873, the daughter of a pious watchmaker named Louis Martin. She was devoutly religious and gained special leave to enter the Carmelite convent at Lisieux when she was only fifteen, taking the name of Sister Thérèse of the Child Jesus and the Holy Face.

The family knew much suffering. Her sister Marie-Hélène died when she was only five, and her mother died from breast cancer when Thérèse was about seven. The child then became very attached to her older sister, Pauline, and was devastated when Pauline left the family home and entered the Carmelite convent at Lisieux two years later. In her autobiography, Thérèse describes her distress at being parted from her sister:

> I started to have a perpetual headache. I think the devil had gained an external power over me, physically; but he was not permitted to invade my soul or my mind. I was so ill that I was not expected to live. I was also haunted by strange fears. My bed was surrounded by terrifying precipices and some nails in the wall of my room took on all the appearance of charred fingers. One day when Daddy was standing beside my bed, his hat in his hand took on the most dreadful shape. And again, for a long time I was unable even to open my eyes.

❖ SHE WAS SO VERY BEAUTIFUL . . .

Many doctors visited the young Thérèse but could do nothing for her. Eventually her father arranged for Mass to be said for her healing at the Sanctuary of Our Lady of the Victories. He also moved into Thérèse's

The spectacular basilica at Lisieux

bedroom a statue of the Blessed Virgin known as Our Lady of the Smile, a favourite of the Martin children who used to shower it with kisses.

On Whitsunday, 13 May 1883, Thérèse recovered. She later ascribed her healing to the presence of the statue: 'Suddenly, the Blessed Virgin appeared beautiful to me. She was so very beautiful. I had never seen anything so attractive. Her face was alive with great kindness and tenderness and she smiled a most ravishing smile. At once all my pain left me and I cried two large tears which slid silently down my cheeks. Yes! I thought, the Virgin has smiled on me. How blessed I am!'

Her sister Marie was there at the time and much later, at the hearings for Thérèse's beatification, she testified to what had happened: 'I saw Thérèse in ecstasy. I knew at once she was looking at no mere statue but that she saw the Blessed Virgin herself. It lasted about five minutes. I knew she would be cured.'

✤ THE WAY OF SPIRITUAL CHILDHOOD

In the convent, several years after her vision, Thérèse seemed quite unremarkable. Shortly before she died she had a conversation with another nun, Mother Agnes. Thérèse said, 'I believe my mission is soon to begin – my mission to teach souls my little way.'

Mother Agnes replied, 'What is this little way by which you would teach souls?'

Thérèse said, 'It is the way of spiritual childhood, the way of trust and complete surrender.'

In her autobiography Thérèse expounded on this teaching:

> It is the way of confidence and abandonment to God. I want to teach the little methods which have proved so utterly successful for myself. It means we acknowledge our nothingness and learn to expect everything from the good Lord – just as a child expects everything from its father. The child worries about nothing but seeks only to gather flowers, and these flowers are sacrifices which it offers to the father for his pleasure. It means we should not be proud of our virtues, for all our goodness – such as it is – comes from God. And we must not be discouraged by our faults. The truth is that children fall frequently.

In 1895 Thérèse developed tuberculosis in both lungs. She suffered terrible haemorrhages and had to be taken from her cell to the infirmary. The statue of Our Lady of the Smile was placed at the foot of her bed.

On 30 September 1897 Thérèse lay dying when suddenly she raised her head from her pillow and gazed in ecstasy at the statue. After a few minutes she sighed, fell back on to the bed and died. Her sister Marie was with her. Later she reported, 'Her stare was held fixed a little above the statue and I saw again that

look on her face she first displayed as a child – all love and adoration – when the Blessed Virgin had healed her. It is impossible to describe, except to say it was something heavenly.'

After Thérèse's death her room in the Martin home was turned into a sanctuary and an altar erected where her bed had been. Copies of the statue were made – one notably by the Trappist sculptor Père Marie-Bernard – and placed in locations where Thérèse had lived, including the infirmary at Lisieux.

A mosaic tile depicting St Thérèse of the Child Jesus

The original statue of Our Lady of the Smile is now in the basilica erected in Lisieux in 1926 following Thérèse's canonization by Pope Pius XI. She has become known as 'The Little Flower' and with Joan of Arc is joint Patroness of France. The shrine to Our Lady of the Smile at Lisieux is one of the best-loved basilicas of the Blessed Virgin in the world.

THE CARMELITES

The Carmelite Order dates from the twelfth century and was an example of the hermit tradition, according to which many adopted a life of solitude and prayer in sacred locations in the Holy Land. The settlement on Mount Carmel in Israel (see p. 104) remains one of the most famous. The traditional robe of the Carmelites is the white mantle, hence their alternative name Whitefriars.

St Teresa of Avila (1542–91) reformed the Order and established convents. The Carmelites are a contemplative Order noted for their commitment to mysticism. One of their most renowned Friars was the great theologian St John of the Cross (1505–60), whose books *The Ascent of Mount Carmel* and *The Dark Night of the Soul* are among the classics of Christian mystical teaching.

✦ VISITING THE SHRINE

Lisieux itself is a picturesque and historic Norman town where from June until October the cathedral hosts a sound and light show portraying two thousand years of Christian history. Thirty-eight impressive steps lead to the entrance of the Romanesque-style basilica; its dome rises almost 100 metres and the interior is decorated with marble and mosaics by Jean and Pierre Gaudin. Thérèse's right arm is preserved in the basilica in a reliquary presented by Pope Pius XI and is displayed every year on 30 September, the day of her death. Each evening from June to September the saint's words are relayed from 9.30 p.m. Visitors should also see Thérèse's family home, Les Buissonets.

The shrine at Lisieux is among the most visited in the world with an annual 2 million pilgrimages. In the Carmelite convent is a wax replica of St Thérèse's body. Her remains have been placed beneath the statue, and relics are displayed for veneration by pilgrims on the last Sunday in September and the festivities continue throughout the week.

Information for Visitors

Location: 18 miles E of Caen in Normandy, accessible from the Channel port of Le Havre. **Contact Numbers:** TEL 31 48 55 08 FAX 31 48 55 26. **Times of Services:** Carmel convent daily 8 a.m., 9 a.m. and 11.30 a.m., basilica Sundays and major festivals 10.30 a.m. and 5 p.m.

St Bernadette

LOURDES

I am the Immaculate Conception . . .

It is more than 150 years since the birth of Bernadette Soubirous, the peasant girl whose visions led to the founding of the shrine at Lourdes in the foothills of the French Pyrenees. Nowadays the site resembles a Christmas grotto in a superstore. Four illuminated basilicas dominate the landscape, there are torchlight processions every day, and the shops are full of statuettes and relics. Five million pilgrims or religious tourists visit every year.

At the time of her vision Bernadette was fourteen years old and barely literate, and had to look after her younger brothers while her mother went out cleaning. On 11 February 1858, while Bernadette was out collecting wood with her sister Toinette and her friend Jeanne, they came to a place where the millstream joined the shallow river by a grotto at Massabielle. The other girls waded through the water, crying because it made their feet so cold. As Bernadette, a sickly, asthmatic girl, held back, she heard what she described as a roar. Later she reported: 'I raised my head and looked towards the grotto. I saw a Lady dressed in white, wearing a white dress, a blue girdle and a yellow rose on each foot, the same colour as the chain of her rosary: the beads of her rosary were white.'

The vision was praying the Rosary. Bernadette took out her beads and did the same. The Lady beckoned but, when the girl dared not approach, she vanished. Toinette and Jeanne saw nothing and at first Bernadette did not tell them what she had seen but they got the story out of her and told her parents. The Soubirous family would not allow her to visit the grotto again, but the girl told her priest, Father Pomian, about the vision and he discussed it with the parish priest of Lourdes, Father Peyramale.

✤ A Vision Called Aquero

On 14 February, a Sunday, Madame Soubirous relented. Bernadette took a bottle of holy water to the grotto and knelt down to say her Rosary. The Lady appeared again. Bernadette said, 'I started throwing holy water at her and told her that if she came from God to stay, and if not to go.' The vision smiled and bowed her head. Bernadette, frightened, threw the rest of the holy water at her and the vision disappeared.

A service in progress at the grotto

On the 18th Bernadette returned once more, this time with two adults, Madame Millat and Antoinette Peyret, 'who advised me to take paper and ink and to ask her, if she had anything to say to me, to be so good as to write it down'. The Lady appeared, said that what she had to say need not be written down, and asked Bernadette if she would come each day for a fortnight. Bernadette began to refer to the vision as Aquero, which means simply, 'It', and said that the Lady spoke in the Lourdes dialect, 'sweet and gentle', and not in French. On this third visit Aquero said,

'I do not promise to make you happy in this world, but in the other.'

According to Bernadette, between 19 February and 4 March 'The vision appeared every day except one Monday and one Friday. She told me several times that I should tell the priests that a chapel should be built there and . . . I should pray for the conversion of sinners. She gave me three secrets which she forbade me to tell anyone.'

Bernadette's account caused mixed reactions. The local police inspector interrogated her and tried to muddle her testimony, but could not: his notes of the interview have been preserved. Some of the villagers were angry at him and threatened to break down the door if he would not release the girl.

The Lady told Bernadette to drink from the spring – a little muddy water that appeared from beneath the rock. Bernadette said, 'I threw it away three times because it was so dirty, but the fourth time I was able to drink it. She also told me to eat a plant that grew in the same place – for sinners – and to crawl on the ground and kiss the ground.'

The Public Prosecutor, Dutour, tried to rig Bernadette's account, but again local men hammered on his door and, trembling, he let the girl and her mother go. Later Bernadette said, 'There was something in me that enabled me to rise above everything. I was tackled from all sides, but nothing mattered and I was not afraid.'

St Bernadette's childhood home in the town

✦ I AM THE IMMACULATE CONCEPTION

At five o'clock on the morning of 25 March, the Feast of the Annunciation of the Virgin Mary, Bernadette felt compelled to go again to the grotto. The Lady was already there. 'With her two arms hanging down, she raised her eyes and looked up at the sky, and it was then that she told me, joining her hands together now at the height of her breast, that she was the Immaculate Conception. Those were the last words she ever said to me.'

Four years before these events, Pope Pius IX had proclaimed the dogma of the Immaculate Conception. For centuries this doctrine – that the Virgin Mary had been conceived and born without the taint of Original Sin – had been a pious belief among the ordinary people; but the proclamation of 1854 had made it part of the Church's official teaching. Controversy surrounded the event, and it is possible that Bernadette had heard angry words flying about in a devout village. But Father Peyramale was convinced by Bernadette's story and became her strongest supporter.

On 3 June, the Feast of Corpus Christ, Bernadette made her First Communion. By the 16th, when Bernadette returned to the grotto, fences had been put up around it and she was obliged to say her Rosary from a distance. When questioned she said, 'I saw nothing but the Blessed Virgin.'

In 1862 a series of interrogations by bishops began. They were impressed by 'her simplicity, candour and modesty, the wisdom of her answers, her calm imagination and commonsense above her age'. To sceptics Bernadette replied, 'I have been told to tell you about it. I have not been told to make you believe it.'

❖ THE VISIONS AUTHENTICATED

Lourdes quickly became a popular shrine and visitors tried to shower Bernadette with money, to steal a relic from her or to cut off a piece of her hood or her dress as a souvenir. She complained of the adulation and said it tired her. Hundreds of letters were addressed to her; she prayed for their senders and asked them to pray for her in turn.

In 1862 the Bishop of Tarbes authenticated the visions and the hard-pressed Bernadette applied to join the St Bernard nuns at Anglet, but was turned down because they did not want to be over-run by pilgrims and tourists. Four things told against her vocation: poverty, fame, poor education and lifelong bad health. In March 1862 Bernadette became very ill and she was given the Last Rites. She recovered to nurse old people in the hospice at Lourdes.

In April 1866 she succeeded in becoming a postulant at Nevers. On her first day she was ordered to recount her visions to the whole community and then never speak of them again. 'I have come here to hide,' she declared. She carried with her three small stones of which she said, 'These are my companions whom I love.' On them she had written the words 'Lourdes', 'The Grotto' and 'Nevers Mother House'. In July she received the habit and became known as Sister Marie-Bernard, but in October she was so ill that she was again given the Last Rites. Once more she defied death, and was later put in charge of the hospital.

In June 1873 she was given the Last Rites for the third time. Yet again she recovered and this time was appointed Assistant Sacristan – the person who kept the chapel clean and in order. But from April 1875 she was a complete invalid, and on 16 April 1879 she died at three in the afternoon – the same hour as Christ's death on the cross.

❖ THE SUFFERINGS OF BERNADETTE

What, apart from this bare chronology, can we know about Bernadette Soubirous? One thing is certain: she strove with all her might to fulfil the vocation announced to her by the Virgin at Massabielle – to do penance, to pray and suffer for sinners. And she did suffer. The Mother Superior at Nevers testified, 'It took her an hour to find a bearable position, during which her face changed and she became as if dead. Even when asleep, the faintest move-ment of her leg made her cry out. Such sharp cries that her companions in the dormitory could not sleep. She shrank to nothing.' In fact, she had tuberculosis. Bernadette did not 'enjoy' suffering, though she spoke of it as 'my job'. And she once said, 'I pray to St Bernard, but I do not imitate him. St Bernard liked suffering, but I avoid it if I can.'

Apart from her physical pain, she bore much personal grief. Her mother died early, at forty-one. Her sister Toinette's first child, also named Bernadette, died in February 1871, to be followed by her father a month later. In fact all five of Toinette's babies died and Bernadette wrote to her: 'I like to imagine that dear little group praying in heaven for us poor exiles on this miserable earth.'

Bernadette suffered, too, from the interrogations of religious historians who tried to make her offer elaborate theological explanations for her visions. But she replied, 'It is best for people to speak and write very simply. It is more moving to read the Passion than to have it explained.'

❖ THE CHARACTER OF ST BERNADETTE

Contrary to popular opinion, saints are not usually 'nice' people and St Bernadette is no exception. The wounds of her childhood poverty and neglect show through her personality and character. Bernadette was said to be of uneven temper, unsociable to strangers, very good at making excuses, too active, stubborn, opinionated, and poor at showing affection. She had particularly difficult relations with Mother Vauzou, her novice mistress, who was well aware of 'two of Bernadette's faults: obstinacy and touchiness'.

The vision's promise – that Bernadette would be happy only in the next life – also seems to have been fulfilled. Bernadette herself felt that she did not respond adequately to Divine Grace and said, 'I am afraid I have received so many graces and profited from them so little.'

Was she even a good nun? On her deathbed she said to the Mother Superior, 'My dear Mother, I beg your forgiveness for all the sorrow I have caused you and for all my failures to keep the Rule. And I beg forgiveness from my dear sisters for the bad example I have given them, especially through my pride.'

In the last stages of her final illness, she requested to be left only with the crucifix sent to her by Pope Pius IX. When she became too weak to hold it, she had it fastened to her breast. After her death she was first beatified in 1925 and then canonized as St Bernadette in 1933.

Is there anything truer or more beautiful, anything more desperately needed in our own violent times, than the heartfelt desire to pray for the forgiveness and salvation of others as well as for ourselves, and to follow the intuitive, undefeated sense and hope in all of us that love and tenderness are the immaculate things in a sullied world? It is not out of place to describe this longing as a vision of the Mother of God.

❖ THE BEAUTY AND WORK OF LOURDES TODAY

Lourdes is justly regarded as the most important place of Catholic pilgrimage in the world after the Holy Land and Rome. It comprises four magnificent basilicas and the grotto marking the exact spot where Our Lady appeared to Bernadette.

It is an awe-inspiring and unforgettable experience for the pilgrim or visitor to join one of the torch-lit processions which begin at the grotto and lead to Rosary Square where the sick are blessed in the name of the Holy Mother. Traditionally there are four gifts of Lourdes: the gift of miraculous water, the gift of healing, the gift of reconciliation, the gift of strength and friendship.

In 1866 the first Mass was offered at the grotto, and on the Feast of the Assumption in 1871 the newly built Church of the Immaculate Conception was blessed. The following year saw the first national pilgrimage, with flags and banners and a torchlight procession. In 1873 the Assumption Fathers organized a much larger pilgrimage and a year later the first visitors came from abroad, particularly from Belgium and the USA. The statue of Our Lady of Lourdes was crowned in 1876 and the second of four great basilicas – the Church of the Rosary – was opened in 1889. On 25 March 1958, the centenary of the apparitions, the Basilica of St Pius X was consecrated.

Pilgrims are invited to sound and slide and video presentations which tell the story of the shrine. Everyone may join in the prayers at the baths. Another moving ritual is the closing of your pilgrimage in the Sheepfold Chapel. There are many other sites and events, some of which are detailed below, but before you leave it is well worth visiting Bartres, the farm where Bernadette worked,

and the parish church where as a young girl she heard Mass.

Every day there is communal anointing of the sick, and there are special services for children and other activities at the nearby Camp for the Young. Discussions and question-and-answer sessions on the subject of the five thousand cures which have taken place are held in the Medical Bureau. Sixty-five of these cures have been officially designated 'miraculous' by the Church.

Wonderfully atmospheric is the nightly procession of the Holy Rosary.

Information for Visitors

Location: 80 miles/130 km SW of Toulouse. Access by air or by coach is provided by numerous religious travel/pilgrimage companies. **Contact Numbers:** TEL 62 42 78 78 FAX 62 42 78 77 INTERNET www.avemaria.org. E-MAIL mail@avemaria.org **Times of Services:** Church of St Bernadette April – October 9 a.m. daily (English), Youth Mass 5 July – 30 August Saturdays 8.15 p.m., Underground Basilica of St Pius X 30 March – 15 October Wednesdays and Sundays 9 a.m. (international). Blessed Sacrament Procession and Blessing of the Sick daily 4.30 p.m. from in front of Adoration Chapel, Torchlight Procession and Rosary daily 8.45 p.m. from Grotto.

OUR LADY OF HOPE
PONTMAIN

My Son will let himself be moved with pity . . .

IN 1870 FRANCE was at a low ebb. The country was at war with Prussia and the Church was in decline. The news, particularly from Paris, was ominous. Prussian troops had surrounded the capital and the sound of shells and cannon-fire was heard every day. Thousands of young Frenchmen had been conscripted into the army, including forty from the little village of Pontmain.

The Barbedette children – Eugène, aged twelve, and Joseph, ten – were altar boys at the parish church and got up early every morning to serve at Mass. Their elder brother, Auguste, was away fighting. On the morning of 17 January 1871 old Abbé Guérin prayed for penitence and courage, and for the special help of the Blessed Virgin in the face of an imminent Prussian attack.

Later that day, just after five in the afternoon, Eugène and Joseph were helping their father with his cows. The three

The Virgin and Child, Domenico Ghirlandaio, 1448-1494

were startled by the sudden appearance of Jeanette Detais, a woman who fulfilled the role of parish messenger but also dressed the dead in their shrouds for burial. Happily, she brought news that Auguste was still alive.

✦ THERE IS A CHARMING LADY!

Much cheered, Eugène went and frolicked in the snow for a while. The sky was like a velvet cloth, covered with stars like pearls. But the boy noticed one completely black area in the sky which he later described as 'like a hole in the heaven'. As he stared at the blackness it filled with a dazzlingly beautiful young woman about seventeen years old, wearing a blue dress and a golden crown.

Joseph looked up, saw the vision too and cried out, 'There is a charming lady!' The boys' father and Jeanette Detais came running to see what the commotion was all about, but saw nothing. Monsieur Barbedette, a kindly man, had no desire to disbelieve his sons; he was mystified and called his wife from the house. Madame Barbedette, less tolerant than her husband, gave them a slap and told them to stop telling lies. But the tearful boys insisted. So she sent for Sister Vitaline, a teacher at the local convent school.

The Sister was prepared to believe the boys' story even though she did not see the apparition herself. 'Sometimes the Blessed Virgin appears only to children,' she said. 'Remember Lourdes. I'll go and fetch some of my girls from the school.' She returned in a few minutes, bringing with her eleven-year-old Françoise Richer and Jeanne-Marie Lebosse, nine. The girls were told nothing but saw the vision at once and corroborated what the boys had said.

A small crowd gathered around the Barbedettes' barn. The adults could see nothing remarkable, but the children joined the visionaries. A babe-in-arms lifted her hands towards the Glorious Mother, as if she wanted to be taken to her breast.

Jeannette Detais went to fetch Abbé Guérin, who stared into the starry night but confessed he could see nothing. The children began to report changes in the apparition: a blue circle around her, a triangle of stars like a medallion, and then a red cross. Abbé Guérin took out his rosary and instructed the people to pray with him. Young Joseph called out, 'The Lady can hear our prayers. She's smiling. There is a banner by her feet!' Slowly and hesitantly, the four children read aloud the words which were being written on the banner: 'Say your prayers, my children. God will soon hear you. And my Son will let himself be moved with pity.'

❖ A CATASTROPHE AVERTED

The villagers fell to their knees and began to sing the Passiontide hymn 'My Sweet Jesu'. At this the Blessed Virgin appeared sad, and the children reported that she now held a larger red Cross with the figure of the crucified Saviour upon it. Four candles appeared around the figure, and the people recalled the memorial candles that were lit every Sunday in church for the men of the village who were away at war. After three hours, during which the form of the vision went through many colourful changes, each one full of biblical symbolism, a veil seemed to cover the Virgin and she vanished.

The following day, news reached Pontmain that the Prussian general had cancelled his attack on their region and withdrawn his troops. Reports declared that some of the Prussian soldiers had been seized with fear because they too had seen the vision. One said, 'A Virgin is shielding the town. We can go no further.' Within less than a fortnight the

> Those who want to prevent their heart from being pervaded by the evils of earth should entrust it to the Blessed Virgin, Our Lady and Our Mother. They will then regain it in heaven, freed from all evils.
>
> ST FRANCIS DE SALES (1567–1622)

Prussians withdrew completely, an armistice was signed and the war was over. Nevertheless it had been a defeat for France. The Emperor Napoleon III was a prisoner and great tracts of eastern France were surrendered to the invaders.

PONTMAIN TODAY

Eugène later entered the priesthood and his brother Joseph joined the Order of the Immaculate Mary. In 1872 the diocesan bishop proclaimed that 'The vision of the Blessed Virgin bears all the marks of a supernatural and divine event', and authorized the building of a shrine. The Barbedettes' barn was converted into a small church, while plans were put in hand for the building of a larger one. When the latter was completed it was declared a basilica and dedicated to Our Lady of Hope. Thirty thousand pilgrims and visitors are drawn to Pontmain every year by the story of the lady who appeared in 'the hole in heaven'.

The basilica is a vast, imposing building with tall towers at the west end. It dominates the little town and can be seen from a great distance around. In front of Our Lady of Hope is a statue of the apparition and to the rear, on the edge of the Park of Calvary, is a museum which tells the story of the events of 17 January 1871.

A most attractive sight is the Chapel of the Lights. The mortal remains of the visionaries and the Abbé Guérin are interred in the cemetery nearby.

In 1996 Our Lady of Hope shrine celebrated the 125th anniversary of the appearance of the Blessed Virgin Mary. Thousands of pilgrims visit each year to pray to the Queen of Peace and Unity.

Information for Visitors

Location: 180 miles/290 km W of Paris and 10 miles/6 km from Fougères. **Contact Numbers:** TEL 43 05 07 26 FAX 43 05 08 25. **Times of Services:** Monday to Saturday 7.30 a.m. and 11 a.m., Sundays 9 a.m., 10.30 a.m., 11.45 a.m. and 5 p.m.

OUR LADY OF THE MIRACULOUS MEDAL

RUE DE BAC, PARIS

O Mary, conceived without sin, pray for us who have recourse to Thee.

THE INSCRIPTION ON THE MIRACULOUS METAL

CATHERINE LABOURE entered the convent of the Daughters of Charity in the Rue de Bac at the beginning of 1830 when she was twenty-four. Since the death of her mother, when the little girl was only nine, she had nurtured a strong devotion to the Blessed Virgin. A woman who had come in to clean the house found the child on top of a chest of drawers in her mother's former bedroom. She was hugging a statue of Our Lady, calling out through her tears, '*You* shall be my Mother!'

✧ THE RUSTLE OF A SILK DRESS

On the night of 18 July 1830, Sister Catherine was sleeping in the convent dormitory when she was awakened by a child's cries. She sat up in bed and saw a little boy of about five standing by the curtain and calling her by name. She later reported that the boy was brilliantly luminous as if lit from within. He told her, 'The Blessed Virgin is waiting for you!' He led her to the chapel, where all the candles and desk lamps were lit

as if for a Festive Mass on a high and holy day, and instructed her to kneel beside the priest's chair in the sanctuary. Twenty-five years later Catherine described the experience in her memoirs: 'I heard the rustle of a silk dress on the other side of the sanctuary. Our Lady bowed before the Blessed Sacrament on the altar and then sat down in the priest's chair. I knelt before her and placed my hands on her knees.'

The Blessed Virgin wept as she described to Catherine the events in store for convents and monasteries, and indeed for all France, in the years to come. 'The times are very wicked. France will be overthrown and the whole world will be beset by evil. Priests will be killed and the Archbishop too. The streets will flow with blood and the Cross will be defiled in a great sacrilege.' Our Lady also had a personal message and a task for Catherine: 'God has a mission for you. It will cause you to suffer greatly but you will overcome through faith.' To Catherine's questions, the Virgin replied that the nature of her mission would be explained later and that the nation's troubles would occur forty years hence. Then the apparition went away as she had come and the little boy led Catherine back to the dormitory.

✦ A SWORD SHALL PIERCE THY OWN SOUL

The next day Catherine told her confessor, Father Aladel, what had occurred but he did not believe her. She was distressed because the Virgin had forbidden her to speak of the events except to Father Aladel. Why had Our Lady commanded her to confide her vision to a sceptic? As the months wore on, the young postulant became increasingly anguished.

Then on the evening of 27 November, when Catherine was at prayer in the chapel with the other sisters, she heard again the rustle of a silk dress. She looked up and saw the Virgin to the right of the altar in a dress of white silk. The vision was standing on a white sphere around which was coiled a snake and in her hands she held a golden orb on which was fixed a Cross.

The Virgin began to scatter precious jewels of all colours which Catherine knew represented graces. After this a medallion appeared, suspended in the air. In her memoirs Catherine wrote, 'It was a large letter "M" with a cross on top and a double bar beneath. Under the letter "M" the sacred hearts of Mary and Jesus were set, side by side. Mary's heart was pierced by a sword and the heart of Jesus wore a crown of thorns.' Catherine would have known well, of course, Simeon's prophecy to the Blessed Virgin when he saw the Christ Child: 'Yea, a sword

PRAYER TO OUR LADY OF THE MIRACULOUS MEDAL

You are blessed among all women! Blessed are you who has believed! The Almighty has done marvels for you! The miracle of the Divine maternity! And, in view of it, the miracle of the Immaculate Conception! The marvel of your *fiat!* You have been so intimately associated to your work for our Redemption, associated to the cross of Our Saviour; your heart was transpierced by it, along with his heart, And now, in the glory of your Son You incessantly intercede for us, poor sinners. You watch over the Church, of which you are the Mother. You watch over each one of your children. You obtain for us, from God, all these graces which are symbolized by the rays of light which radiate from your open hands. With the one condition that we dare ask you for them, and that we draw near to you with the confidence and the simplicity of a child. And it is, in this way, that you bring us constantly towards your Son Jesus.

PRAYER OF POPE JOHN PAUL II,
31 MAY 1980, RUE DE BAC

shall pierce through thy own soul also' (Luke 2 : 35). The Virgin instructed Catherine, 'Have a medallion made after this pattern.'

Catherine went again to Father Aladel, who was still sceptical. On three more occasions Our Lady appeared to her, and at the last visitation expressed dismay that the medallion had not been made. The young nun returned to Father Aladel and told him that the Virgin was displeased. For the first time the priest began to wonder whether Catherine was more than just a pious dreamer.

In autumn 1831 Father Aladel called on the Archbishop of Paris and told him the story of the medallion. The Archbishop, impressed, gave orders that it should be made. Meanwhile, Catherine had been transferred to a hospice at Enghien as a cook.

✤ THE VIRGIN'S MEDALLION AND SCAPULAR

Father Aladel arranged for 1500 medallions to be made by an engraver in Paris called Vachette. They featured on one side an image of the Virgin, and on the reverse a symbol combining the cross with the letter M. Beneath the M were two hearts and around it twelve stars. All the Sisters of the convent of the Daughters of Charity were given a medallion, and when she received hers Catherine said, 'I shall wear it worshipfully. The main task now is to make it widely known.'

The medallions became so popular that by the end of 1836 two million of them had been distributed in France. The 'M' soon came to stand for 'miraculous' as reports spread of cures and blessings received by those who wore one.

Meanwhile Catherine kept her promise to the Virgin not to speak of her apparitions to anyone but Father Aladel, even when challenged.

The Blessed Virgin had also told Catherine that she desired a statue and an altar to be placed in the chapel where she had appeared, and these things had not been accomplished. In 1876, when Catherine was seventy, she went in tears to the Mother Superior, Sister Dufes, and told her that she was the nun who had seen the visions. At once Sister Dufes commissioned a sculptor to make a statue, but Catherine did not live to see it as she died of heart disease on the last day of that year. She was placed in an open coffin where, in death, her face regained the bloom of youth.

Sister Catherine was beatified on 28 May 1933 and declared a saint on 27 July 1947 when her body was discovered to be miraculously preserved. It was moved back to the chapel on the Rue de Bac where she had received her visions and where a new altar now stood in fulfilment of Our Lady's command. The statue stands over and behind the high altar, under an arch inscribed with an invitation for pilgrims to come on foot and receive all the blessings of Our Lady. The Virgin, in white marble, stands on a rock. She wears a golden crown and has a halo of twelve stars. From her open hands stream rays of golden light symbolizing the graces she brings for all humankind.

Another tradition at Rue de Bac is that of the green scapular. On 28 January 1840, the novice Justine Bisqueyburu received a vision of the Virgin in which Our Lady asked her to distribute the green scapular. Justine did so.

The words printed on the scapular read, 'Immaculate heart of Mary, pray for us now and at the hour of our death'.

Our Lady told Justine that the scapular would procure many conversions to the faith and physical healings. The distribution of the scapular was first approved by Pope Pius IX in 1863.

More than a million pilgrims visit Rue de Bac every year. Miraculous medals can still be purchased at the Convent shop. A full programme of services operates throughout the day.

Information for Visitors

Location: 140 Rue de Bac, 75340 Paris Cedex 07. **Contact Numbers:** TEL (1) 49 54 78 88 FAX (1) 4954 78 89. **Times of Services:** weekdays 8 a.m., 10.30 a.m., 12.30 p.m. (in addition Tuesdays only 4 p.m. and 6.30 p.m.) Saturdays 5.15 p.m., Sundays 7.30 a.m., 10 a.m. and 11.15 a.m. Pilgrims accompanied by their own priest may arrange to celebrate Mass with the shrine authorities. Marian Devotions 4 p.m. daily. Chapel open weekdays 7.45 a.m.–1 p.m. and 2.30–7 p.m., Sundays 7.20 a.m.–1 p.m. and 2.30–7 p.m.

OUR LADY WITH THE GOLDEN HORSE
ALTÖTTING

To the Queen of Heaven, Virgin of Altötting, whose holy house is the foundation stone of the Bavarian Dynasty.

PRINCE MAX JOSEF, FROM A PARCHMENT IN THE HOLY CHAPEL

ALTÖTTING IS A town in Bavaria which, when the Roman Empire collapsed, was the centre of a region occupied by the Teutonic Bajuvari tribe. The most famous chieftain of this tribe was Otto. Just before AD 700 St Rupert was engaged in missionary work in the area and preached to Otto, who expressed his heartfelt desire to be baptized. There was no church for the ceremony and so St Rupert consecrated a local pagan shrine – a seven-sided temple, serving the cult of the planets – for the purpose.

Following the end of Roman rule Altötting – 'Old Otto's Town' – became part of the Holy Roman Empire. In 876 Emperor Charles the Bald founded a Benedictine monastery there which flourished under his patronage. A few years later Altötting was attacked by warlike tribes thrusting westwards and looking for living space in the rich lands of central Europe. The invaders pillaged most of the town and the monastery, but spared the seven-sided chapel which contained a statue of Our Lady given, according to legend, by St

Rupert. In 913 Duke Arnult finally defeated the invaders in a fearful battle fought on the outskirts of the town at a place subsequently called Mordfeld – the field of death.

The Benedictines controlled the chapel until Duke Lewis replaced them in 1228 with a company of lay canons. A new Romanesque style church was completed in 1244 and became a renowned place of pilgrimage, especially during the Black Death. Many came to Altötting and prayed to the Blessed Virgin to be spared the Plague.

✣ THE PILGRIMS' WOODEN CROSSES

Soon a larger church was needed to accommodate the thousands who came to worship, so a yet more splendid building was completed in 1511. The old chapel was preserved and was surrounded by a circular cloister which remains to this day, providing a walkway for visitors from which they can see into the shrine itself. Each pilgrim takes one of the wooden crosses placed in the entrance and carries it on his or her walk through the cloister as an act of penitence.

Among the most striking features of the shrine are the series of medieval pictures which depict the baptism of Otto, and the Tablets with Miraculous Pictures, portraits of those granted miraculous cures by Our Lady. Within the shrine itself are interred the hearts of many of the emperors, princes and dukes of the Holy Roman Empire.

The interior of the shrine is a haven of soft, velvety, restful darkness in contrast to the sudden brilliance of the eastern niche which is solid silver from roof to floor. On the altar is a wooden statue known as Our Lady's Image, carved in the thirteenth century as a replacement for the original presented by St Rupert, now lost. The smiling, crowned Madonna holds the Christ Child on her right arm. She wears a blue and pink dress bordered by gold and holds a sceptre; at her breast is a ruby brooch. This is one of the finest of all the ancient statues of Our Lady. The faces of both Madonna and Child have been turned black by centuries of candle-smoke, a tribute to the continuous worship at the shrine.

The eighteenth century was a time of political turbulence in Europe, and the rise of secularism and republicanism resulted in the suppression of many religious Orders. The Jesuits, who had come to Altötting in 1591 and built a monastery, a Church of St Mary Magdalene and a hospital, were expelled from Altötting in the late eighteenth century, and their dismissal was followed by that of the Franciscans in 1803. But Catholic restoration gathered pace as Napoleon's power waned, and the Emperor Josef II himself went to Altötting in 1814 to offer thanks to the Blessed Virgin for this deliverance.

✣ OUR LADY WITH THE GOLDEN HORSE

Visitors to the shrine queue to see the magnificent figure of Our Lady with the Golden Horse in the treasury. Made in the early fifteenth century of solid gold, it is regarded as one of the finest pieces of medieval goldsmith's work in Europe. It depicts a Virgin and Child surrounded by angels and children, and at her feet is a little lamb among flowers made of gemstones.

Altötting has prospered over the centuries from rich endowments made by many kings and popes until it has become one of the most magnificent shrines of Our Lady anywhere in the world. More than two million pilgrims and visitors attend each year, and at least four thousand Masses are said in the Holy Chapel.

Information for Visitors

Location: 55 miles/88 km E of Munich on German–Austrian border. **Contact Numbers:** TEL (86) 71 5166. **Times of Services:** weekdays 6–10 a.m. on the hour every hour.

THE CHAPEL OF MERCY
KEVELAER

Here, thou shalt build me a chapel.

THE BLESSED VIRGIN TO HENDRICK BUSMAN, CHRISTMAS 1641, AT KEVELAER

CLOSE ON three-quarters of a million pilgrims come to the small village of Kevelaer each year. Historically it was a tragic place, almost completely destroyed by fire in the late sixteenth century. The remains of the old village made an eerie sight on the desolate moorland, and it was certainly not a place where people paused. The country round about was further ravaged in the Thirty Years' War of 1618–48.

In 1641 a mysterious event took place on the site of the original village and this was reported to the Synod of Venio by a travelling tinker from the neighbouring town of Geldern.

My name is Hendrick Busman . . . At Christmas in 1641 I was making my way in the course of my business from the town of Weeze when I came to the region around Kevelaer. There was a cross by the roadside and there I heard a voice saying to me, 'Here thou shalt build me a chapel.'

I heard the voice and looked about me but saw no one. I resolved to press on and put all thoughts of the phenomenon out of my head. About a week later, I passed the place again and there heard the same voice

speaking the same words as before. I heard it again, a third time. I was sad because I was poor and I had no means by which I might build a shrine. Nevertheless, I saved regularly from my petty cash in the distant hope that one day I should have a fund to fit the purpose.

Then, four weeks before Whitsun, my wife Mechel received a vision by night. She saw a great light and in the midst of it a shrine; and in that shrine was a picture of Our Lady of Luxembourg like one she had been shown some time earlier by two soldiers passing through our village. The soldiers had offered to sell Mechel the picture but, upon asking the price, she realised she could not afford it.

When Mechel told me of her vision, I connected it with my own experiences near Kevelaer and I urged her to find the soldiers and the picture. She discovered that the picture was now in the possession of a lieutenant presently in prison in Kempen. Mechel obtained the picture from him . . .

Hendrick tried to construct the shrine following Mechel's description. When the Carmelite nuns at Geldern heard of his experiences they asked him to give them the picture for safe-keeping. The nuns venerated the image in an unbroken twenty-four-hour vigil and then, at his urgent request, gave it back to Hendrick. But the Busmans' house was then so overrun with visitors and pilgrims that Hendrick asked the Capuchin monks to store the picture in their chapel. Again huge crowds gathered to pay homage to the image.

Hendrick managed to build a little shrine at Kevelaer and had the picture delivered there in solemn procession to the parish priest. Father Johannes Schink was at once overwhelmed by the sheer numbers of pilgrims who came to venerate the picture, and the bishop sent three priests to help him in his stewardship of the little shrine. Immediately there were reports of cures and special blessings. The Vicar-General ordered an official commission, and within a very few years declared that the cures were indeed miraculous.

DAS GNADENBILD VON KEVELAER

The image known as Our Lady of Luxembourg

❖ ROSES AND IMAGES IN GOLD

In 1654 the original brick pillar central to Hendrick Busman's first shrine was incorporated within a new and larger sanctuary. A plaque at the base of the old pillar bears the names of Hendrick and Mechel and pays tribute to them as the founders of the devotional cults to Our Lady, Comforter of the Afflicted.

The 1654 sanctuary contains the altar on which the miraculous image now sits in the place of honour. The picture is a copy of the famous Luxembourg statue of Our Lady, Consoler of the Afflicted, a Madonna and Child carved in limewood. The six-sided shrine, called the Chapel of Mercy, is topped by a modest steeple and stands in the square known as the Kapellenplatz. Next to the original shrine is the Candle Chapel.

This is where most of the processions end. Every day a hundred candles burn during the singing of the vesper, 'Praise be to the Madonna'. There is a Renaissance nave and a breathtakingly beautiful baroque high altar which features an image of Our Lady in white and red.

Well worth a visit is the nearby Priests' House which is the oldest stone building in Kevelaer and the organisational centre for the shrine. In front of the Confessional Chapel is the Fountain Courtyard where water bubbles ceaselessly over the inscription, 'The grace of God flows eternal'.

Many pilgrims make the procession of the Stations of the Cross which are set in a large park opposite the Klarissen Nunnery. The route is tree-lined and peaceful and it leads at last to the Park of Mary where there is a large statue of the Virgin.

A highlight among a very full programme of Sunday and daily services is the 10 a.m. Sunday Mass accompanied by choir and orchestra.

The square is now dominated by a huge basilica built in honour of the Virgin and to accommodate the great number of pilgrims.

The famous picture itself is only 12 centimetres tall and 8 centimetres wide, and features the crowned Madonna holding the Infant Jesus. It is set in a gold frame decorated with angels and roses and images in gold provided by north German princes. The picture was officially crowned in 1892, 250 years after the shrine's inauguration.

After Altötting, Kevelaer is the most famous of all the Marian shrines in Germany. Pope John Paul II made a personal pilgrimage there in the 1980s. It is a magical place, still set among the original cobbles from the time when Hendrick Busman received his joyful summons to build a shrine in a desolate location.

Information for Visitors

Location: 35 miles/56 km NW of Düsseldorf. **Contact Numbers:** TEL (283)2 93380 FAX (283)2 70726. **Times of Services:** St Mary's Basilica: Saturdays 6.30 p.m., Sundays 7.15 a.m., 8.30 a.m., 10 a.m. (sung with choir and orchestra), 11.30 a.m. and 7.30 p.m., weekdays 10 a.m. Pilgrim Sermon, 3 p.m. Pilgrim Sermon and Devotions. Pax Christi Chapel: Sundays 10.15 a.m. Confessional Chapel: weekdays 6.30 a.m., 8 a.m. and 6.30 p.m., Saturdays 6.30 a.m. and 8 a.m. Grace Chapel: Saturdays 8 a.m. Mass for Peace, (*Friedensmesse*). Candle Chapel: weekdays 6.30 p.m. Mary-Praise and Pilgrim Devotions. Chapel of the Blessed Sacrament: weekdays 9 a.m., 2–5 p.m. Silent Worship.

— IRELAND —

OUR LADY QUEEN OF IRELAND

KNOCK

REPUBLIC OF IRELAND

Our Lady of Knock, Queen of Ireland, you gave hope to your people in a time of distress and comforted them in sorrow . . .

FROM THE PRAYER TO OUR LADY OF KNOCK

ON THE EVENING of 21 August 1879 Mary McLoughlin, housekeeper to the parish priest in Knock in County Mayo, was astonished to see the outside south wall of the church bathed in a mysterious light. She also saw three figures standing in front of the wall, which she thought were replacements for ones recently destroyed in a storm. Mary rushed through the rain to the house of her friend Margaret Byrne.

✣ THE VIRGIN IN A YELLOW CLOAK

After half an hour Mary decided to leave. Mary Byrne, Margaret's sister, aged twenty-nine, said she would walk home with her. As the two women passed the church, they both saw clearly an amazing vision. Mary Byrne later described the experience:

About three hundred yards or so from the church, I saw all at once, standing out from the gable and to the west of it, three figures which, on more attentive inspection, appeared to be the Blessed Virgin, St Joseph and St John.

The figure of the Virgin was life-size, the others apparently not so big or not so tall. They stood a little way from the gable wall as I could judge, a foot and a half or two feet from the ground. The Virgin stood erect with eyes raised to heaven, her hands elevated to the shoulders or bosom. She wore a large cloak of white colour hanging in full folds and somewhat loosely gathered around her shoulders and fastened to the neck. She wore a crown – rather a large crown – and the cloak appeared to me somewhat yellower than the dress or robes worn by Our Blessed Lady.

Mary McLoughlin stood her ground and stared fixedly at the apparition, while Mary Byrne ran home to tell her family what she had seen.

Soon a sizeable crowd gathered, and all saw the apparition. The parish priest, Archdeacon Cavanagh, did not come out, however, and his absence was a source of disquiet and disappointment to the devout village folk.

Among the witnesses were Patrick Hill and John Curry. As Patrick later described the scene: 'The figures were fully rounded, as if they had a body and life. They did not speak but, as we drew near, they retreated a little towards the wall.' Patrick reported that he got so close as to make out the words in the book held by the figure they all supposed to be St John.

An old woman called Bridget Trench drew very near and tried to embrace the feet of the Virgin, but the figure seemed always just beyond reach. Others out in the fields and some distance away saw a strange light around the church. The vision persisted for two or three hours and then faded.

❖ THE ARCHBISHOP'S TESTIMONY

The next day a group of villagers went to see Archdeacon Cavanagh, who accepted the genuineness of their report and wrote to the diocesan bishop of Tuam. The Church authorities set up a commission to interview a number of the people who had claimed to see the apparition.

The diocesan hierarchy was not convinced, and some members of the commission ridiculed the visionaries and alleged that they were victims of a hoax perpetrated by the local Protestant police constable! But ordinary people were not so sceptical, and the first pilgrimages to Knock began in 1880. Two years later Archbishop John Joseph Lynch of Toronto made a visit to the parish and claimed he had received personal healing from the Virgin of Knock.

In due course, many of the original

Crowd praying at Knock Shrine, Co. Mayo c. 1880

witnesses died. But Mary Byrne married, raised six children and lived the whole of her life in Knock. When interviewed again in 1936 when she was an old woman of eighty-six her account did not vary from the first report she had given on that rainy night back in 1879.

❖ THE VISIT OF JOHN PAUL II

The village of Knock was transformed by the thousands who came to commemorate the vision and to say prayers for healing for others as well as for themselves. The local church could hold six hundred and was large for a village of sixty or seventy people. Even so, it had to be extended to accommodate the throng of pilgrims and sightseers. In 1976 a new church, Our Lady Queen of Ireland, was built. It holds more than two thousand and needs to, for each year more than one and a half million visitors arrive to pay respects to the Blessed Virgin.

The Church authorities gradually relaxed their scepticism, and in 1971 the Sacred Congregation for Worship declared that the anointing of the sick and the dying might be performed at the shrine. However, there has still been no statement of formal approval from the Tuam diocese, despite the fact that Pope John Paul II made a personal pilgrimage in 1979.

A recent memorable day for Knock dawned in June 1993 when Mother Teresa visited the shrine.

The busiest period for pilgrimages is from May to the end of October and there are all-night vigils which anyone may attend on the first Fridays in May, June, July, August, September, October and December. The Feast Day of Our Lady of Knock is celebrated on 21 August – a wonderful festival occasion attended by many thousands of pilgrims who crowd into the Solemn Masses and join the procession which commemorates the apparition of 1879.

The shrine is open all year round and there are daily guided tours. Remember to walk the way of the Stations of the Cross and to visit the folk museum. The shrine is easily accessible for wheelchairs where occupants are given places of honour in the church during mass.

In 1994 three life-size statues commemorating the original apparitions were erected behind a glass screen. They are of Our Lady, St Joseph and St John. Majestic and imposing, these figures contribute a tremendous sense of presence to the shrine.

Information for Visitors

Location: Co. Mayo in NW of Republic of Ireland. Access by air from London. Trains and buses to Ballyhaunis (7 miles/11 km away) from Dublin and Belfast. **Contact Numbers:** TEL (94) 88100 FAX (94) 88295. **Times of Services:** 27 April–12 October weekdays 8 a.m., 9 a.m., 11 a.m., 12 noon, 3 p.m., 5 p.m. and 7.30 p.m., Sundays and Holy Days 8 a.m., 11 a.m., 12 noon, 3 p.m. and 7 p.m., eve of Sundays and Holy Days 7.30 p.m.

OUR LADY OF LOURDES
MONEYGLASS
NORTHERN IRELAND

In the ages to come, when we who have raised it to God's glory shall be forever passed and gone, it may still endure as a sign of our faith, as a monument of our trust in God and as a testimony of our deep devotion and confidence in the Ever-Blessed and Immaculate Mother.

FATHER JOHN O'NOLAN, PARISH PRIEST OF MONEYGLASS 1913–30

THE MASSIVE foundation stone for the new church of Our Lady of Lourdes at Moneyglass was cut from the mountainside at Lourdes in 1920. It was then transported to the Grotto, where the Bishop of Lourdes celebrated Mass for all those who had contributed to its building costs. The stone was received in Belfast by Father W. P. Lagan of St Peter's Church and placed on the gospel side of the sanctuary, where it is always in view of the priest celebrating Mass at the high altar. The new church was intended to be 'the nation's tribute to Our Lady of Lourdes' and as such it was dedicated in August 1925.

After the building of the church, the next step was the construction of the National Grotto of Our Lady of Lourdes. The first sod was cut in October 1926 in the presence of an immense throng. The parish priest, Father O'Nolan, said that the Grotto would be 'the special audience chamber of Our Lady', and it was meant to be as like the original one at Lourdes as possible. Thirteen metres wide, ten

feet deep and rising to a height of thirteen metres, the new Grotto could accommodate more than a hundred worshippers to hear Mass. The altar and pulpit rails were copies of those at Lourdes.

The square in front of the Grotto, abutting the new church, was large enough to accommodate five thousand people on major festivals. A Calvary was erected at the rear of the Grotto, approached by thirty-three stone steps recalling the years of Our Lord's life.

The stonework of the Grotto is impressively sturdy and from a niche above the main entrance a statue of the Virgin, hands clasped in prayer, looks down to welcome pilgrims and visitors.

❖ THE PENAL CROSS OF MONEYGLASS

The church was reordered in 1992 according to the criteria for places of worship proposed by the Episcopal Liturgical Commission of

The Grotto where pilgrims can attend Mass

Christ while he was being scourged, the ladder, the superscription of his accusation, INRI, and the lance with which the soldier pierced his side.

At the bottom of the Cross are carved a skull and crossbones and the intriguing symbol of a cockerel and a pot. According to Irish tradition, Judas Iscariot's wife assured him that Christ would no more rise from the dead than the cockerel would rise from the boiling pot into which she had placed him. Whereupon the cockerel rose from the cauldron, flapped its wings and cried, 'The Son of the Virgin is safe and well!'

 ## THE SHRINE TODAY

Apart from the regular services, Mass is celebrated at the grotto on several announced occasions during the year. The parish priest is always pleased to hear from people wishing to visit or arrange pilgrimages.

The renewed and re-ordered interior of the church has been especially designed to facilitate lay participation in the Liturgy in accordance with the innovations in worship declared by the Second Vatican Council.

Ireland: 'A church differs from other buildings in that it is first and last a work of faith and a sign of faith. The major focal points of the liturgy, namely the altar, the chair, the ambo, the tabernacle, the font and the confessional, serve their immediate function.'

A feature of the church is the Moneyglass Cross, carved after an ancient design by D. McSorley at the time of the reordering. The traditional design of these Irish so-called 'Penal Crosses' – after the era of Catholic persecution during which most of them were made – is unusual. They depict the dice with which the Roman soldiers cast lots for Our Lord's robes at the Crucifixion, the hammer and pliers, three nails, the cords which bound

---

Information for Visitors

Location: Moneyglass is NE of Toome, Co. Antrim. **Contact Number:** TEL (01648) 50225. **Times of Services:** Monday, Wednesday and Friday 7.30 p.m., Saturday 7.30 p.m., Sunday 10 a.m.

THE MADONNA AND CHILD

MOUNT CARMEL

This special devotion to Mary is historically verified and explicitly affirmed. At the moment of choosing for themselves a patron, in prompt fulfilment of a prescription given to them in 1209 by Albert, Patriarch of Jerusalem, the Carmelite Friars had not the slightest hesitation: they chose Mary.

FATHER NILO GEAGEA, 1995

MOUNT CARMEL overlooks the coastal plain and the ancient road from Egypt to Damascus, and its strategic siting has made it the scene of many battles. Only a few miles to the south-east lies the old, ruined city of Megiddo, a place sacked, destroyed and rebuilt more times than any other settlement in the world between 1469 BC, when Thothmes III of Egypt defeated the Canaanites, and 1918 when Field Marshal Allenby put paid to the Turks towards the end of the First World War. Megiddo is the place name from which is derived Armageddon, the location for the Last Battle and the end of the world as prophesied in Revelation 16.

Carmel was also the dwelling-place of the first and greatest of the Jewish prophets, Elijah, who lived there in a cave in the ninth century BC and defeated the pagan prophets of Baal. Many stirring legends are told of Elijah: of how he called down fire from heaven to the dismay of his enemies, how he was fed by ravens and, most sensationally of all, how he did not die but was taken up into the presence of God in a chariot of fire. But it is a story concerning Elijah's vision of the Blessed Virgin which inspired the Christian Carmelite Order (see p. 80), who since the twelfth century have worshipped here.

This tradition says that when Elijah saw the cloud 'no bigger than a man's hand' which brought rain to ease the protracted drought in Israel, it contained a vision of the Virgin Mary. John the Baptist of St Alexis, who built the first monastery on the plateau of the Carmel headland, relates how God revealed to Elijah in the cloud the Immaculate Conception. He tells also the legend of Our Lady's visits to the Cave of Elijah, brought there by her parents, Anne and Joachim, when she was a girl; and of how Our Lord, as an infant, took refuge in the Cave of Elijah with Mary and Joseph when they were returning to Nazareth after their escape into Egypt.

OPPOSITE The dramatic setting of Carmel Heights

✤ THE TRIBULATIONS OF MOUNT CARMEL

The Carmelite Order was initiated towards the end of the twelfth century when some Western pilgrims settled on the mountain and lived austere, penitential lives in the cave there. These first monks showed a profound devotion to the Blessed Virgin and made her Patroness of the Order. The Carmelites observed a very strict rule which included abstinence from meat and a prolonged fast from 14 September (the Feast of the Exaltation of the Cross) until Easter!

When the Crusades made life dangerous in the Middle East, the Carmelites left their monastery and settled in various places in the West: in Cyprus, Messina, Marseilles, Genoa and at Aylesford in England. The few friars who remained behind were massacred by the invading Muslims under Al-Ashraf Khalil on 30 July 1291.

A few friars returned to Mount Carmel, at least as visitors to the ancient shrine, but there was no lasting Carmelite presence there for centuries. In 1631 the Spanish monk Prosper of the Holy Spirit obtained permission to rebuild the monastery and in November that year he celebrated Mass in the Cave of Our Lady. There were constant squabbles with their Muslim neighbours and life was so hazardous that the friars kept guard dogs and firearms for self-defence! In 1799, during the Napoleonic Wars, the monastery was seized by the French and used as a military hospital.

In the nineteenth century relations between Christians and Muslims improved and a full restoration of the monastery was attempted. A new church was dedicated in

June 1836. At the beginning of the First World War the friars were expelled by the Turks, who sacked the monastery on the pretext that it was being used as an arms depot. The Vatican appealed to the Turks and secured the concession that friars might continue to live in the monastery so long as they submitted to German/Turkish authority. A company of German soldiers was stationed on Carmel until its liberation by Australian troops in September 1918.

On the eve of the Second World War the monastery was requisitioned by the British army, who mined the slopes and restricted the operation of the lighthouse which had been built there in the 1920s. After the war, violence between Jews and Arabs drove many families in the nearby port of Haifa to seek refuge outside the city. The friars took in all refugees and let them occupy the ground floor of the monastery. At the end of the British mandate in Palestine in 1948 the Israeli army took over Mount Carmel and used the lighthouse as their naval officers' HQ. In 1959 the American Secretary of State, John Foster Dulles, appealed to the Israeli authorities who agreed to give the monastery back to the Carmelites.

✣ PEOPLE OF MANY FAITHS

Catholic seminarians from the College in Rome now make annual visits to the monastery, which also provides retreats for Christians of many denominations living in Haifa. Israeli soldiers are frequent visitors to the Cave of Elijah, a source of national and military inspiration. Catholics and Muslims often join one another for prayer, especially on 20 July, the Feast Day of Elijah. There is a well-established Carmelite Pilgrims' Centre to accommodate the thousands who visit one of Christianity's most ancient sites and a focus of devotion to Our Lady.

The magnificent statue of the Blessed Virgin in the monastery church, carved by the Genoese sculptor Giovanni Battista Garaventa in 1820, was crowned in the Vatican in 1823 in the presence of Pope Pius VII and solemnly enthroned on Mount Carmel in 1836. In 1932 the clothes of the statue were carved in wood. Our Lady wears an expression of exquisite tenderness as she sits crowned on her throne with the Infant Jesus upon her left knee. Her dress is all blue and gold and two cherubs support her footstool.

The two largest events of the year are held in the summer. On 15 July is the Festival of Our Lady of Mount Carmel and there is an atmospheric commemoration of the prophet Elijah on 20 July. This is held in Elijah's Grotto, an important part of the shrine dedicated to the prophet's original prevision of the Blessed Virgin.

— ITALY —

OUR LADY DELLA GUARDIA

GENOA

Come to me at della Guardia, and I will restore you!
OUR LADY TO FATHER GIUSEPPE MARIA SABELLI, 1727

BENEDICT PAVETO was a shepherd in the Ligurian mountains of north-west Italy. On 29 August 1490 he was out on the mountain-side cutting grass, waiting for his wife to bring his lunch, when he was startled by a dazzling light in the middle of which was a vision of the Madonna and Child. Benedict was terrified and fell to his knees. The Virgin spoke to him: 'Do not be afraid. I am the Queen of Heaven and I have come to ask you to build a church in this place.'

Benedict answered that he was a poor man and did not think he could ever find the resources. 'Trust me', the Virgin replied. The shepherd watched as the apparition slowly faded, and then ran back home down the hillside towards his house. On his way he met his wife, who mocked him and said he must be suffering from sunstroke.

✤ OUR LADY SHOWS MERCY TO BENEDICT

The following day Benedict climbed a fig tree to pick the fruit, but the branch to which he was clinging snapped off and he fell. Friends carried him home, where it was discovered that he had broken bones and severe internal injuries. They sent for the priest and Benedict was given the Last Rites. In appalling pain, he promised that he would build a church to the Blessed Virgin if she would save his life.

The Virgin appeared again, scolded him for his lack of faith and said his fall was a punishment for allowing his wife to persuade him that his vision had been an illusion. Our Lady stretched out her hand towards him and, when Benedict's friends and neighbours saw that he was healed, they believed his account of the apparition.

A church was built on the hillside and it became so popular that it was quickly extended and then rebuilt. In 1583 the shrine was visited by the Bishop of Novarra, who commended the people for their piety and especially praised the high altar and the image of the Blessed Virgin carved on it.

In 1604 a commission of inquiry into the apparitions was opened by the Archbishop of Genoa. The shrine was authenticated, given the name Madonna della Guardia – Our Lady of the Guard-post – and became one of the chief centres of Marian devotion in Italy. The Confraternity of Our Lady of the Rosary was established there in 1598 and in 1614 a Company of the Glorious Virgin of Carmel was founded.

✦ A WONDERFUL DELIVERANCE

Our Lady della Guardia was accredited with the deliverance of Genoa from the invading army of Charles Emmanuel, Duke of Savoy, in 1625. There was an Order of Capuchins in the city and one of them, Fra Tomaso da Trebbiano, urged the citizens to pray to Our Lady della Guardia. Next day, when Charles's huge army marched confidently towards the city, it was repulsed by a few hundred poorly armed locals inspired with religious fervour.

In gratitude the people erected a belltower at the shrine, and on the Feast of the Assumption in 1632 a marble statue of the Blessed Virgin was set up over the high altar. In 1654 della Guardia became the first Marian shrine to institute the ritual of the Solemn Coronation of Our Lady, a joyful ceremony in which thousands of pilgrims climbed to the top of the hill, sang and prayed as the crown was placed on the head of the marble statue.

Many miraculous cures associated with Our Lady della Guardia have been officially authenticated. In 1727, for instance, Father Giuseppe Maria Sabelli was dying of tuberculosis. He was half paralysed and highly feverish when he heard Our Lady call out to him, 'Come to me at della Guardia and I will restore you.' On 26 July, the Feast of St Anne,

his friends carried him up the mountain and laid him in the church to receive the Blessed Sacrament. As he lay there he heard a melodious voice: 'Stand up! I am the physician who has healed you. Let everyone know you are well again'. Father Giuseppe stood up and everyone saw that he was completely cured.

The basilica of della Guardia was built in 1923, and the greatest day in its calendar is 29 August when there are colourful celebrations to commemorate Benedict Paveto's original vision. The walls of the church are inlaid with marble and near the high altar is the perpetually lit Niche of Our Lady which displays her crowned statue.

The anniversary of the first apparition, 29 August, is a most spectacular occasion with brilliant illuminations which turn night into day. To join in the torchlight procession is a moving and unforgettable experience.

Information for Visitors

Location: Genoa is Italy's largest port in the NW with good road, rail and air links.
Contact Number: TEL (10) 71 8010. **Times of Services:** daily 4 p.m., feastdays 8 a.m., 9 a.m., 10 a.m., 11 a.m., 12 p.m., 4 p.m. (winter), 5 p.m. (summer). 29 August is the Feast of the Apparitions with illuminations and a torchlight procession.

OUR LADY OF THE ROSARY
POMPEII

He who propagates my Rosary shall be saved.

THE WORDS OF THE BLESSED VIRGIN TO BARTOLO LONGO, OCTOBER 1872

AS YOU DRIVE south along the coast road from Rome to Naples, the Apennine mountains loom high and hazy on the left, while to your right is the warm Mediterranean, sparkling blue and silver in the dazzling Italian sun. The German writer Goethe (1749–1832) made a tour of Italy during which he exclaimed, 'I have never seen true daylight before!' As you approach Naples, you are treated to two spectacular sights: the great bay where once the most powerful fleet of warships in the world was anchored; and, colossal in mist and smoke, the active volcano Vesuvius.

✦ A PRIEST OF THE DEVIL

The modern Italian town of Pompei was built about eight miles/13 km away from the ancient Roman city of Pompeii, destroyed in the famous eruption of AD 79, and in the eighteenth and nineteenth centuries it was infamous as the haunt of robbers and brigands. Yet it became the setting for one of the most astonishing visitations of Our Lady.

Bartolo Longo (1841–1926) was a Naples lawyer who was introduced to Satanism while still a young man. He was ordained a priest of the Devil and rose to high rank in the Church of Satan where daily, by preaching, incantation and the Black Mass, he scorned and reviled the Catholic Church and took pleasure in blaspheming the names of Jesus and Mary. But Bartolo is a wonderful example of the truth that no one, however depraved, is beyond the loving reach of God. Through the prayers and counsel of a friend, Vincente Pepe, he was converted to the Christian faith and lodged with a Dominican friar named Alberto Radente. Bartolo sought to atone for his sins by joining a local group who ministered to the sick and poor.

One day in October 1872, he was walking in open country near Pompeii when his mind was clouded by a sudden dread. He was oppressed by recollections of his evil deeds in the Church of Satan and wondered if he would ever be entirely free from their consequences. Years later he wrote down his feelings at that time.

I knew that the Priesthood of Christ is for all eternity and so I conjectured that the

The basilica of the Church of Our Lady, Pompeii

Priesthood of Satan is similarly unending. So, even though I had repented, I thought I might still be bound to the Devil and that, as his slave, I was bound to find him waiting for me in the fires of hell.

As I brooded on these things, I felt a profound despair and I was determined to do away with myself. Suddenly, I seemed to hear an echo of Friar Alberto's voice, repeating the words of the Blessed Virgin to St Dominic: 'He who propagates my Rosary shall be saved.'

These words brought light to my soul. I fell to my knees and called out, 'If your words are true, then I shall be saved. I shall not leave this world before I have propaga-ed your Rosary.' At once the bell of the parish church of Pompeii rang out to call people to the Angelus. It was like a signature to my promise.

❖ A COARSE COUNTRY WOMAN

Bartolo immediately arranged a mission to the whole parish and asked the priests involved to teach the meaning of the Rosary. He also determined to exhibit a picture of the

Blessed Virgin and told Friar Alberto, who informed him that a certain nun, Mother Concetta, had such a painting in her convent. Bartolo went to see it but was disappointed. He wrote: 'It was torn and worm-eaten and the face of the Virgin was that of a coarse country woman. The other figures in the painting were hideous. St Dominic looked like a tramp or an idiot. Well, I had promised a picture for that same evening so, with great reluctance, I took it.' Mother Concetta assured him that the Holy Mother would work miracles by it.

The picture was too big and heavy to carry, so he arranged for a waggoner to deliver it for him. The man happened to be transporting a cartload of manure to a field near Pompeii, and that is how the Queen of Heaven arrived in the city on 13 November 1875. Bartolo arranged for the picture to be restored and improved in time for the inauguration of the Confraternity of the Holy Rosary which he had set up. He also launched an appeal for the building of a church to house the picture.

During the building of that church Mother Concetta's prophecy of miracles was fulfilled. The foundation stone was laid on 8 May 1876. One month later Giovannina Muta, lying in bed dying of tuberculosis, had a vision of the painting of Our Lady. A ribbon seemed to fall towards her out of the picture, bearing the words: 'The Virgin of Pompeii grants your requests.' Giovannina was instantly cured. Twelve-year-old Clorinda Lucarelli was cured of violent epilepsy; then Concetta Vasterilla, a woman at death's door, was restored to health; finally, Father Anthony Varone, who was dying of gangrene, was made completely well again. Father Varone preached and celebrated at Mass on the day after his cure, the Feast of the Holy Rosary.

✧ THE ROSARY GIVEN TO ST DOMINIC

Bartolo worked hard providing for orphaned children and writing about the history and meaning of the Rosary. In 1885 he married the widowed Countess Mariana di Fusco: the couple devoted themselves to the care of the orphans and paid for the training of forty-five ordinands.

The Church of Our Lady of Pompeii was consecrated by Cardinal La Valletta, representing Pope Leo XIII, in May 1891. In 1934 Pope Pius XI declared that a basilica should be built, which now houses the portrait of Our Lady of the Rosary in a golden frame. The Holy Mother sits on a throne with the Christ Child on her knee. Jesus is depicted delivering the Rosary to St Dominic, while Mary is seen handing it to St Catherine of Siena. The portrait, which arrived on a load of manure, had been ornamented over the years with so many jewels that they were damaging the picture, so the jewels now form a separate display. The picture is adorned only with a crown of diamonds donated by the congregation after restoration in 1965.

A new book of the thoughts and writings of Bartolo Longo has recently been published and it is available at the shrine. It contains the visionary's reflections on such topics as the Rosary, the Shrine, Faith, Charity and Prayer, as well as a section devoted to Our Lady.

✤ VISITING THE SHRINE

While in Pompeii don't miss the spectacular view from the 80-metre belvedere. There is an elevator and the tower is open 9 a.m–1 p.m. and 3–5 p.m.

Ten thousand pilgrims attend the shrine every day. On 8 May, the Feast of the Holy Rosary, more than one hundred thousand meet to say the prayers written in honour of Our Lady by the penitent Bartolo. The bodies of Bartolo and Mariana are laid to rest in the crypt of the great basilica. On 26 October 1980 Bartolo was beatified by Pope John Paul II – a demonstration that, however far a sinner may stray, he can be retrieved by the love of the Holy Mother.

Information for Visitors

Location: just S of Naples. **Contact Numbers:** TEL (81) 850 7000 FAX (81) 850 3357. **Times of Services:** weekdays every hour 7 a.m.–noon, 4 p.m., 5 p.m. and 6.30 p.m.; 6 p.m. Rosary. Sundays and Holy Days every hour 6 a.m.–1 p.m., 4 p.m., 5 p.m., 6.30 p.m. and 7.30 p.m., also (in the crypt) every hour 8.30 a.m.–12.30 p.m.

OUR LADY OF MONTALLEGRO

RAPALLO

I am Mary, the Mother of God. Tell the people of Rapallo that this my picture was brought from Greece to this mountain by angels.

THE VIRGIN IN A VISION TO GIOVANNI CHICHIZOLA, 2 JULY 1557

Montallegro, 'The Happy Mountain', rises above Rapallo on the Italian west coast south of Genoa. In the sixteenth century the port was under constant threat of Turkish invasion and a series of battles was fought, the most famous of which was Lepanto in 1571.

✤ CHAINED TO A ROCK

Fourteen years earlier a peasant farmer named Giovanni Chichizola, from Canevate in the mountains, was working on Montallegro. As he sat down to rest at midday, he heard a voice calling him by name and a mysterious

The sacred ikon showing Our Lady asleep on a bed with the Holy Trinity standing guard

herself at the moment of her Assumption into heaven, and told him that this image had been brought by angels from Greece. She also instructed him to fast on Saturdays. When the apparition had gone Giovanni tried to pick up the picture and take it home with him, but it was fastened securely to a large rock. There were other farm workers nearby and Giovanni called to them to come over. Then a stream of water began to run from beneath the rock to which the picture was attached.

Giovanni ran down the mountain into the town and told his story to the priests. Some of them laughed at him, but others, accompanied by a group of curious onlookers, went back up the mountain with Giovanni. They managed to detach the picture from the rock and carried it in solemn procession to the parish church in Rapallo where it was placed under lock and key.

Astonishingly, according to legend, when the archpriest went to look at the picture the following day it had vanished. It was later discovered back on the rock where it had first appeared. Everyone interpreted this as a clear indication that Our Lady wished the picture to remain on the mountain, so they built a shrine to house it. Crowds attracted by the story began to make their way to Montallegro, and many sick people were cured when they drank from the stream. A permanent church, which involved tremendous excavations in the rocky terrain and the transportation of huge quantities of materials up the mountain, was built within the year.

The picture itself is about 15 centimetres by 12 and features Our Lady asleep on a bed. Beside the bed are depicted the Holy Trinity:

light seemed to be suspended before him in the air. As he turned to look more closely, he saw the figure of a lady standing beside him. She said, 'Don't be afraid, Giovanni. I am Mary, the Mother of God. Tell the people in Rapallo that you have seen me.'

The Virgin showed Giovanni a picture of

God the Father, Son and Holy Ghost. There are also angels and an apostle, almost certainly meant to be St Peter. These figures are clothed in traditional Greek vestments, confirming the apparition's words to Giovanni about the picture's origin.

✦ THE SPRING TURNS RED

The vision had said that the picture was brought to Italy by angels, but in 1574 some sailors who had been saved from a shipwreck climbed Montallegro to offer thanks for their deliverance at the shrine of the Blessed Virgin. At once the captain claimed to recognize the picture as one that had been stolen from his home town, Ragusa (Modern Dubrovnik), in 1557, the year in which it had first appeared to Giovanni Chichizola. The captain took the issue to court and was awarded possession of the picture. Legend says that the picture once again miraculously returned to its place on the rock in the church on Montallegro.

Meanwhile an official inquiry had begun into the events on the mountain and subsequent claims of miracles, and its findings are stored in the provincial library at Genoa. Several times, it was attested, the city was saved from the plague, and it was also asserted that the spring had turned red during a war with France in 1625. In 1739 the district was permitted to name Our Lady of Montallegro as its Patroness, and in 1767 she received her Coronation.

✦ THE ROCK OF THE MIRACULOUS IMAGE

The church, designated a basilica, stands some 2165 feet/660 metres above sea level. It is a three-hour walk from the bay below or a 10–30-minute ride by cable car, depending on the weather; whether you walk or ride, the views are spectacular. The picture is displayed in a highly ornamented reredos behind the high altar.

The original rock upon which the picture appeared is built into the structure of the basilica. On one side of the altar is a basin in white marble into which runs water from Giovanni's spring, and above the basin a little door leads to the Rock of the Miraculous Image of the Assumption. Water pours continually from this hidden source, and over the centuries containers full of it have been carried by pilgrims to the four corners of the earth. In 1950 a new hostel and a retreat house were built to provide accommodation and hospitality for pilgrims and visitors.

Among the most important festivals at Rapallo is the commemoration of Nostra Signora di Montallegro, held during the first three days of July and featuring a dazzling fireworks display.

Information for Visitors

Location: 15 miles/24 km SE of Genoa.
Contact Number: TEL (18) 5 239000.
Times of Services: weekdays 10.30 a.m., Sundays 8.30 a.m., 10 a.m., 1 p.m.

SALUS POPULI ROMANI
SANTA MARIA MAGGIORE, ROME

Let us ask the Blessed Virgin to nominate an heir.

THE PATRICIAN JOHN IN ROME BEFORE THE MIRACLE OF THE SNOW IN 352

A WEALTHY aristocrat and devout Christian known by tradition as John lived in Rome in the fourth century. He and his wife had no children, and were fearful that their lack of an heir would put an end to the family's long prominence in the government of the city. They had often prayed for a child but without success. One day John's wife said, 'Let us ask the Blessed Virgin to nominate an heir.' They did so, and their prayer was answered dramatically.

✦ SNOW IN AUGUST

In August 352 a rectangle of snow was discovered on Mount Esquiline, one of the famous Seven Hills. Snowfall of any sort was unheard of in Rome at that time of year, but that it had fallen only in one place and in such a specific pattern was regarded as a phenomenon. People crowded to see the patch of snow, which persisted despite the heat. John was convinced that its shape and size indicated that a church should be built on the spot. In fact both John and Pope Liberius had dreamt that Our Lady desired a church to be built on Mount Esquiline. The Holy

Father was so moved by his dream that he visited the mysterious snowfall. When he arrived with his retinue, John and his wife were already there kneeling in prayer to the Virgin.

As soon as the plot for the building had been staked out the snow melted. John met the cost of the building, which was completed in 354 and was dedicated the Basilica Liberiana. Seventy years later the church was rebuilt on a grander scale by Pope Sixtus III, who added decorations and ornaments of silver. From then the church was known as Basilica Sixti and the Church of Santa Maria Maggiore (St Mary Major).

✦ THE PRODIGY OF THE SNOW IS TRUE

The new basilica housed a celebrated painting provided by Pope Liberius. It had belonged to St Helen, the mother of the Emperor Constantine – the same Helen who, according to tradition, had made a pilgrimage to Palestine and discovered the original Cross of Christ. The picture, painted on a slab of cedar wood, is of a Madonna and Child. The infant

Jesus is holding a book and both figures are haloed and crowned – the crowns presented by Pope Gregory XVI in 1832 as a thank-offering for deliverance from cholera.

The so-called 'new' Lady Chapel was built by Pope Paul V in 1613 to house the miraculous painting. He declared, 'This image should have a magnificent place of its own, befitting its eminence. For it has always been regarded by all faithful people and through it many miracles and wonders have been wrought.'

Salus Populi Romana (Salvation of the Roman People) is the title of this famous painting and it is rightly named because for centuries the people of Rome have prayed before it in times of famine, war and national crisis.

Many popes have held the basilica on Mount Esquiline in particular regard. When Gregory I was Pope (590–604) Rome was ravaged by a plague. Gregory carried the image of the Holy Mother in procession from the chapel as far as Hadrian's Mausoleum. When the procession arrived they heard an invisible heavenly choir singing *Regina Coeli*. When the Pope asked the Virgin to pray for the city he saw an apparition of St Michael replacing the sword of vengeance in its scabbard. The plague abated.

OPPOSITE PAGE The magnificent interior of the Church of Santa Maria Maggiore

Miraculous fall of snow, Mino da Fiesole

Pope Benedict XIV had a special affection for the legend. In 1427 he declared, 'It must be acknowledged that nothing is wanting to enable us to affirm with moral certainty that the prodigy of the snow is true.' Benedict XVI attended the holy picture every Saturday and prayed the Litany. The night before he died, Paul V asked to be taken to the Chapel of the

Blessed Virgin in order to pray before her image. St Ignatius Loyola, founder of the Society of Jesus, said his first Mass here at Christmas 1538.

✤ ANGELS SING THE RESPONSES

The Chapel of the Virgin Salus Populi Romani (Protectress of the Roman People) is very close to the historic heart of the Catholic Church, so it is not surprising that many stories have enriched its tradition over the centuries. It is said that once when Pope Gregory the Great was celebrating Mass in the chapel and intoning the words '*Pax Domini sit semper vobiscum* (The peace of the Lord be always with you)', he heard a choir of angels sing the response '*Et cum spiritu tuo* (And with thy spirit)'. From that day the custom in the chapel was to omit that section of the Mass in the belief that it was being offered and sung by the angels.

✤ THE BASILICA TODAY

The present-day church is one of the largest basilicas in the world and its Patronal Festival is held on 5 August in remembrance of the miracle of the snow. During this celebration hundreds of white blossoms are showered from the dome of the chapel. Not to be missed are the thirteenth-century mosaics on biblical themes and the frescoes by Reni and Della Porta. There is an imposing Roman-esque belltower erected in 1377.

Santa Maria Maggiore has a further claim to fame. In the seventh century a relic was brought from Bethlehem and traditionally

venerated as the manger in which the Christ Child was laid at the first Christmas. And so another name for the great basilica is St Mary of the Crib.

One of the most spectacular sights which meets today's pilgrim is the triumphal arch which extends to almost 66 feet/20 metres. It is decorated in four horizontal sections. In the middle at the top God's throne is set in a circle, with St Peter and St Paul on either side. Above this mosaic are the symbols of the four gospel writers.

On 12 November 1964 Pope Paul VI made a pilgrimage to the basilica and solemnly proclaimed Our Lady 'Mother of the Church'. He prayed: 'With a spirit full of trust and filial love, we raise our glance to you, despite our unworthiness and our weakness. You who have given us Jesus the source of

Information for Visitors

Location: central Rome in the Piazza Santa Maria Maggiore. **Contact Numbers:** TEL (6) 488 1094 FAX (6) 4890 4392. **Times of Services:** daily at 7 a.m.; 8 a.m., 9 a.m., 10 a.m., 11 a.m., 12 noon, 6 p.m., Holy Rosary and Litany of Our Lady 5.30 p.m., Exposition of the Blessed Sacrament from 9 a.m. – 5 p.m.

grace will not fail to help your church at this time when she is flowering because of the abundance of the gifts of the Holy Spirit and in committing herself with renewed zeal to her minim of salvation.'

The Mass at 10 a.m. on Sundays and on major festivals is always a Solemn Mass sung in Latin.

In addition to the regular services, Masses are allowed in any language to all groups of pilgrims, preferably accompanied by their own priest. One week's advance notice is requested.

Confessions are heard in almost all languages from 7 a.m. – 12 noon and from 4 p.m. – 7 p.m.

THE WEEPING MADONNA OF SYRACUSE, SICILY

'Will men understand the mysterious language of those tears?'
POPE PIUS XII IN A RADIO BROADCAST ON 17 OCTOBER 1954

IN TUSCANY IN the early 1950s, a sculptor called Amilcare Santini suddenly felt compelled to mould a plaque depicting the Immaculate Heart of the Blessed Virgin. He completed the work in three days, varnished, painted and polished it and fixed it to a black opaline panel. The heart was 30 centimetres high. Because it was made from a mould, it was no trouble to mass-produce many others. Amilcare distributed his holy plaques in many Italian cities, where they were purchased as gifts appropriate for a Confirmation or First Communion.

One of the plaques was bought as a wedding present for Angelo and Antonia Iannuso, who were married early in 1953.

They placed the Immaculate Heart on the wall over their bed. The newly-weds could not afford a home of their own and went to live with relatives in Syracuse. Soon Antonia was suffering a difficult pregnancy during which she developed toxaemia and suffered fits which turned her temporarily blind. In the early hours of 29 August, one of these fits came on and she lost her sight. It was restored at about nine o'clock in the morning. Later, she wrote down what happened:

> I opened my eyes and gazed at the image of the Madonna above our bed. To my astonishment I saw that the effigy was weeping. I called to my sister-in-law, Grazia, and my aunt, Antonia Sgarlata.

When they came in I showed them the tears. At first they thought it was an illusion on account of my illness, but when I insisted, they went closer to the plaque and saw for themselves that tears were really falling from the eyes of the Madonna. Some of her tears had run down her cheeks and on to the bedhead. They were afraid and they took the plaque out by the front door and called the neighbours who also saw the phenomenon for themselves.

✤ AN ALTAR IN THE STREET

Mario Messina, a highly respected local man, was sent for. He examined the plaque closely, dried it and observed that the tears reappeared at once. The plaque was placed on an outside wall because so many people were clamouring to see it. Even so, the crowds were seen as a threat to public order and so it was removed to the police station. When the officers saw that the Immaculate Heart no longer wept, it was taken back to the house.

The image continued to weep throughout the following day, a Sunday, and local people came to collect the tears on strips of cloth and lace handkerchiefs. Many people claimed that they were instantly healed of their illnesses. The plaque was then set up on a temporary altar in the street as crowds gathered to pray the Rosary.

A commission comprising senior clergymen, scientists and local worthies was appointed to examine the plaque thoroughly. The Immaculate Heart continued to weep. The surface of the effigy was found to be completely smooth with no holes or pores,

and when the backing was removed the inside was perfectly dry. Still the image wept. A small sample of tears was taken for chemical analysis at a local laboratory. The report declared: 'The appearance, the alkalinity and the composition suggest that the liquid examined is analogous to human tears.' At 11.40 a.m. on 1 September the tears ceased.

✤ THE MYSTERIOUS LANGUAGE OF TEARS

Many senior clerics visited the Iannusos and examined the plaque. The Archbishop of Syracuse recited the Rosary with the family, and in December the Archbishop of Palermo gave his official judgment: 'After careful sifting of the many reports and after noticing the positive results of the strict chemical analysis which examined the tears, we have unanimously announced the judgment that the reality of the facts cannot be in any doubt.'

The speed of this proclamation was sensational because, in the interests of ruling out fraud and malpractice, the Church generally takes years to authenticate apparitions. Often no approval is given, even

---

Mary is an arsenal of grace and she comes to the aid of her clients. She sustains, strengthens and revives us by the heavenly favours that she heaps on us.

ST PAULINUS (353–431)

---

where there are scores of reliable witnesses. It was therefore almost a miracle when Pope Pius XII announced on 17 October 1954: 'We acknowledge the unanimous declaration of the Bishops' Conference held in Sicily on the reality of the event. Will men understand the mysterious language of those tears?'

Within a few years the official medical commission considered almost 300 reported miraculous cures and declared that 105 were 'of special interest'. Antonia Iannuso made a complete recovery and gave birth to a son on Christmas Day 1953.

The events in Syracuse received sensational worldwide publicity in the media. Even sceptics confessed that they had observed the weeping, and the phenomenon was captured in photographs and on film. The scientists who examined the plaque declared that the occurrence was 'extraordinary'.

❖ SANTUARIO MADONNA DELLE LACRIME

The tears collected for scientific analysis were placed in a reliquary presented to the Archbishop of Syracuse. Inside is a crystal urn in which the tears themselves have now crystallized.

The Iannusos' house in the Via degli Orti is now a chapel where Mass is celebrated regularly in commemoration of the Weeping Madonna. A shrine was built and dedicated as the Santuario Madonna delle Lacrime. Thousands of pilgrims come each year to kneel before the reliquary of the Immaculate Heart of Mary.

The miraculous events at that little house are in a long tradition of the Weeping Madonna which goes back to the time of Our Lord's Crucifixion when, in the words of St Bonaventura, '*Stabat Mater Dolorosa*' – His mother stood there, weeping.

Information for Visitors

Location: on E coast S of Catania. **Contact Numbers:** TEL (9) 31 21446 FAX (9) 31 65379 **Times of Services:** weekdays 6.30 p.m.; Sundays 6.00 p.m. and 7.00 p.m.

— JAPAN —
THE HOLY MOTHER OF AKITA

Veneration is due to the Holy Mother of Akita. Her messages are the same as those delivered at Fatima in 1917.
BISHOP ITO OF NIIGATA, 22 APRIL 1984

AGNES KATSUKO SASAGAWA was born in Akita in 1931. The birth was premature and Agnes was always a frail child. When she was nineteen she went into hospital to have her appendix out and, through a mistake with the anaesthetic, was paralysed. After ten years' immobility, during which time she was looked after by a Catholic nun, Agnes made a sudden spontaneous recovery and as an act of thanksgiving was baptized.

❖ A WHITE LIGHT AND A RED FLAME

In May 1973 she entered the convent of the Handmaids of the Eucharist in Yuzawadai, a suburb of Akita. One month earlier she had been suddenly afflicted with total deafness. Agnes now stood before the altar and opened the tabernacle which housed the Blessed Sacrament. As she did so, a glorious white light shone from the altar. Agnes, overwhelmed, fell to her knees and remained in

prayer for a whole hour. The experience was repeated the following day.

On 14 June Agnes saw the glorious light shining out of the tabernacle again and it seemed to hold a red flame. When she told the other sisters of her vision, they accused her of spiritual arrogance and forbade her to talk about it. She continued to experience the apparition of light almost daily, and on more than one occasion it was accompanied by a vision of angels.

Eventually she could keep quiet no longer and, while Bishop Ito was on a pastoral visit to the convent, told him about her visions. The Bishop told her to remain calm, to give herself fully to the routine of the spiritual life and to wait for God's guidance.

❖ I AM YOUR GUARDIAN ANGEL

At the beginning of July Agnes felt a severe pain in her left palm. When she examined it she saw a wound in the shape of a small cross.

The weeping statue at Akita

sins, but those of all humankind. Remember that the Sacred Heart of Our Lord is always wounded by the sins and the ingratitude of the world. Remember too that the wounds of the Virgin Mary are deeper than yours.'

Suddenly, Agnes saw standing beside her a glorious figure which smiled and said, 'I am your guardian angel.' The angel led her to the chapel and then disappeared. Agnes knelt before the tall wooden statue of Our Lady, which was bathed in a sudden brilliant light. The Virgin spoke: 'Daughter, you have shown me obedience in giving up all to devote yourself to my service. I know you suffer a great deal because of your deafness, but you will be cured. Only be patient. Pray for the sins of the whole world.'

Next morning Agnes asked Sister Kotake to inspect the statue, and the other nun saw a bleeding wound in the wooden hand. Agnes's own wound came and went in a regular pattern: it appeared on Thursday evenings, grew worse on Fridays and disappeared each Sunday, as if in commemoration of the passion and death of Christ. On 26 July, the Feast of St Anne, the Mother of the Virgin Mary, Agnes's wound was more painful than ever and at the same time the statue in the chapel began to bleed more profusely. She went again to the Bishop and

The mistress of the novices, Sister Saki Kotake, bandaged her hand and told her that the wound had been sent by God. Unable to sleep, Agnes got out of bed at three in the morning and knelt to pray. She heard an inner voice: 'Don't be frightened. Pray ardently for the forgiveness of sins – not just your own told him of her suffering and misery. He advised her to consult a doctor, but first Agnes went to the chapel to pray for strength.

Here she heard the voice of the angel once more: 'Our pain will come to an end today. Pray to the Sacred heart and the Precious Blood. Pray for the sins of the whole world. Tell the Bishop that the blood is shed today for the last time.' At once the pain left her and the wound in her hand was healed. The statue also ceased its bleeding at the same time, though the imprint of the wound remained in the wood.

❖ THE SCENT OF FLOWERS

On 3 August Agnes was praying in the chapel near the statue of the Virgin when she heard the voice of the Holy Mother: 'If you love the Lord, you will listen closely to my words. Many souls in this world hurt and offend the Lord. I am looking for souls who will console Him. God the Father is preparing a great chastisement which will be poured out on all humankind. Only prayer, penitence and asceticism can turn away the Father's wrath. Obedience is the foundation of all things.'

On 29 September, St Michael and All Angels' Day, Agnes and another nun were in the chapel when the statue of Our Lady suddenly blazed with light. The other nun saw this vision too and said, 'Look, the wound in the statue's hand has healed!' That evening the two nuns noticed that the statue of the Virgin was oozing liquid, and the angelic voice said to Agnes, 'Our Mother is even sadder than before. Dry her tears!' The liquid had the scent of flowers and it persisted for seventeen days.

On 13 October 1973, the Virgin gave Agnes another message warning of terrible events to come, and saying that this was the last time Agnes would hear her voice. Two days later when the nuns went into the chapel they were met by a terrible stench and found white worms all over the floor. Next day the worms were gone but the smell remained. It had been faintest in the confessional, but after a few days it had all dissipated.

❖ AGNES ACCUSED

During Benediction on 13 October 1974, the fifty-seventh anniversary of the last apparition at Fatima (see p. 141), Agnes's hearing was restored as Our Lady had promised her. Delighted, she telephoned Bishop Ito.

On 4 January 1975 one of the nuns ran to the office of their chaplain, Father Yasuda, to tell him that the statue had begun to shed tears once more. The weeping was extraordinarily lifelike and occurred more than a hundred times, finally ceasing on 15 September 1981, the Feast of Our Lady of Sorrows.

A few weeks after the weeping began, samples of tears, liquid and blood were taken from the statue by Professor Eiji Okuhara of the biochemistry department at Akita University. Without stating where they had come from he passed them to a colleague, a non-Christian forensic expert named Dr Kaoru Sagisaka, who examined them and reported: 'The matter adhering to the gauze is human blood. The sweat and tears absorbed in the pieces of cotton are also of human origin.'

News spread and the little convent received many pilgrims and a great deal of media attention. On 6 March 1975, Agnes's deafness returned. She was examined by two doctors who both felt she would never hear again.

That year Bishop Ito opened an official inquiry into the weeping Madonna and appointed a leading Marist scholar, Father Garcia Evangelista, to chair it. In May 1976, Father Evangelista reported that the substances produced by the statue were not of supernatural origin: 'The fact is that Sister Agnes, whose diaries I have read, is a medium. The blood, tears and sweat are produced by her ectoplasmic powers and mediumistically transferred to the statue.' That month he preached a week's retreat at Akita while Agnes was away visiting her dying mother. In one of his sermons Father Evangelista described Agnes as 'a psychopathetic case' with a split personality. The nuns were despondent.

At Bishop Ito's instigation a second inquiry was set up via the Apostolic Delegate, but unfortunately Father Evangelista was appointed to head this one too. Summoned to Tokyo to be interviewed by him, Agnes was told that she had confused and misled many people and had accepted money from newspapers for articles about her visionary experiences.

✤ AGNES VINDICATED

Bishop Ito was not satisfied and was perturbed by the effect of both inquiries' findings on the spiritual life of the sisters. He decided to go to Rome and discuss his disquiet with the Sacred Congregation for the Doctrine of the Faith, who informed him that it was within his jurisdiction to appoint a new commission of inquiry and that he himself, as diocesan bishop, should be a member.

In due course this third commission declared by a majority of four to three that the events at Akita were of supernatural origin. There had already been one report of an associated miracle. A Korean woman, Teresa Chun, claimed to have been healed of a brain tumour after sleeping with a photograph of the Weeping Madonna by her pillow.

On 1 May 1982 Agnes's guardian angel told her that she would again have her hearing returned, this time permanently. It happened on the Feast of Pentecost, 30 May. The doctors who had previously diagnosed her as incurably deaf could offer no explanation for this remarkable occurrence.

At Easter 1984 Bishop Ito issued a pastoral letter to the whole diocese declaring the happenings at Akita to be of supernatural origin. He said that veneration was due to the Holy Mother of Akita and that her messages had been the same as those delivered to the children at Fatima sixty-seven years earlier. Now the little convent at Akita is a centre for international pilgrimage. In 1988 Cardinal Ratzinger of the Sacred Congregation declared that the apparitions had been authentic revelations of the Divine.

✤ THE CONVENT

The little convent itself is a plain, low building in the modern Japanese style, set in a garden of prayer, which contains a statue of the

Virgin on a rock beside a pond. Inside, the convent is panelled in light-coloured wood which matches the replica of the famous statue *Our Lady of All Nations*. The parquet floor is a golden colour. There is a tall fireplace in two colours of Japanese brick and above it hangs a picture of Pope John Paul II next to another of the Immaculate Heart of Mary and the Sacred Heart of Jesus, both set in a frame of mother-of-pearl. A larger shrine is being built. The entrance to the garden is known as the Gate of Heaven. Another area, the Garden of the Lamb, is set apart for meditation and prayer. Here also are the Stations of the Cross which were blessed and dedicated on 18 August 1994.

There is a packed schedule of services and devotions every day. The sisters highlight the daily Mass at 6.40 a.m. and the 7.30 a.m. Mass on Sundays. Also on Sundays, Rosary at 4.30 p.m. is followed immediately by Evening Prayer, Adoration and Benediction.

Information for Visitors

Location: on NW coast of Honshu Island about 280 miles/450 km N of Tokyo. **Contact Numbers:** TEL (188) 68 2139 FAX (188) 68 4728. **Times of Services:** Monday to Saturday 5.30 a.m. Morning Prayer, 6.10 a.m. Eucharistic Adoration, 6.40 a.m. Holy Mass, 11.10 a.m. Rosary, 11.45 a.m. Noon Prayer, 5 p.m. Rosary, 5.35 p.m. Evening Prayer, after dinner Night Prayer. Thursday night after dinner Holy Hour (Eucharistic Adoration), Saturday morning Confession. Sundays 6.30 a.m. Morning Prayer, 7.30 a.m. Holy Mass, 11.45 a.m. Noon Prayer, 4.30 p.m. Rosary, followed by Evening Prayer/Adoration, Benediction; after dinner Night Prayer. Lent 4.30 p.m. Stations of the Cross.

— MEXICO —

OUR LADY OF THE ROSES

GUADALUPE

Behold a miraculous cloak, strewn with roses, in the form of a portrait of the glorious Mother!

BISHOP DON JUAN DE ZUMARRAGA

IN THE MID-SIXTEENTH century a middle-aged man named Juan Diego was living in the village of Tolpetlac by Lake Texcoco on the outskirts of the old Aztec capital, Tlatelolco. The Aztec nation had recently been destroyed by the Spanish Conquistadors and European Christianity had been introduced into the New World. On 9 December 1531 Juan, a baptized Native American, was walking over the loaf-shaped hill of Tepeyac to Mass in Tlatelolco. He prayed silently as he walked, remembering his wife who had died three years earlier, and he was sorrowful because they had had no children.

✦ BUILD ME A REFUGE

As he reached the summit he saw a white cloud surrounded by a rainbow and heard beautiful music. He wondered if the place was haunted, or if he was hearing the song of some strange bird. A woman's voice arose, melting in its tenderness and calling him by name. Finally he saw her: a young woman,

glorious, smiling at him, surrounded by the rainbow. He fell to his knees.

'Juanito,' she said, addressing him by the customary pet name for children called Juan, 'where are you going so early in the morning?' He replied in the same childlike idiom: 'My Lady and my little child, I am walking to Tlatelolco to hear Mass there.'

The Lady said, 'Then know and believe in your heart of hearts that I am Mary, holy and perpetual Virgin . . . I desire above all things that you build for me here a holy place, a refuge, so that I may show my love and pity for your people. Believe me, I am your Mother and the Mother of all humankind. Those who love me and seek me I will comfort. Here in this place I will answer their prayers and heal their sorrows. You must go to the Bishop of Mexico and tell him these things.'

Juan set off straightaway for the house of the Most Reverend Don Juan de Zumarraga in the capital. The servants were astonished at the audacity of a mere peasant who came

A typical street scene outside the basilica

demanding to see the Bishop at such an early hour, but the Bishop was already at work and Juan was admitted to his presence.

Zumarraga was patient but sceptical. He knew that the hill of Tepeyac had been the site of a temple to Tonantzin, the old Aztec corn goddess. He also thought Juan was over-excited and that, given time, his vision would fade. He told his visitor to come and see him again in a few days' time. Juan left downhearted.

As he again reached the summit of Tepeyac, the vision reappeared. He fell before her, weeping and confessing his failure. 'Blessed

Mother,' he cried, 'perhaps you should look for someone more persuasive than I to convince the Bishop of Mexico!' The Virgin smiled and replied, 'No. I have chosen you, my son.'

Juan was thus encouraged to return the next day to convince the Bishop. Zumarraga told him to bring some proof that he had really seen a vision of the Holy Mother, and that she had commanded him to build her shrine. Juan promised him a miracle.

As the Indian left, the Bishop had him followed. But on Tepeyac hill he eluded his pursuers and merged into the spiritual realm inhabited by the Virgin Mother. With a tender smile she said, 'Very well: the Bishop shall have his miracle tomorrow!' Juan ran home full of happiness.

But his joy turned to sorrow when he discovered that his uncle, the only family he had left, was dying. The Virgin had asked Juan to return to the hill the following day, but he decided that his duty was to be with his uncle.

❖ THE CASTILIAN ROSES

On the morning of 12 December Juan's uncle begged him to go to the Santiago monastery at Tlatelolco and arrange for him to be brought the Last Rites and the Blessed Sacrament. Juan was fearful of meeting the Virgin, for he had broken his promise, so he took a long detour. But suddenly in the open country she stood before him and asked where he was going and why he looked so sad.

When he told her his story and begged her understanding and forgiveness she replied, 'Don't worry – your uncle will not die. In fact he is already well again. Now go to the top of Tepeyac hill and you will find Castilian roses growing there. Pick some of them and bring them back to me.' Juan was astonished to find roses in full bloom on the mountaintop in winter. He took handfuls of them down the slope to where he had met the Virgin, who concealed them inside his cloak and told him to show them to the Bishop.

Zumarraga listened patiently because he was curious to see what the Indian was clutching so firmly under his cloak. At last Juan loosed the garment and a few roses fell to the floor – but the great abundance of them remained inside his open cloak in the form of a portrait of the Blessed Virgin. The Most Reverend Don Juan de Zumarraga, Bishop of all Mexico, fell to his knees in awe before the image. It was only then that Juan saw for himself the full glory of the heavenly portrait. The Bishop had his miracle. Zumarraga took the cloak to his private chapel where he laid it before the altar of the Blessed Sacrament.

❖ THE DEAD MAN RAISED

Next day Juan, the Bishop and his entourage set off over Tepeyac hill and Juan showed his companions where the Virgin had appeared to him. When he eventually arrived back at his own house he found his uncle up and about, bursting with health. He too had received a vision of the Virgin. He said, 'She came here and told me of the shrine she requires on Tepeyac. She said it should be dedicated to Holy Mary of Guadalupe. But I don't know what that means.'

But the Bishop knew what it meant: Our Lady of Guadalupe was an old Spanish statue of the Blessed Virgin. Zumarraga kept his promise and arranged for a little church to be built near the summit of Tepeyac. On 26 December the image of the Virgin made of roses on the cloak of Juan Diego was carried to the new church with great solemnity and rejoicing.

Tradition has it that a miracle occurred there. The Mexicans, as was their custom, arranged a mock battle as part of the celebrations. One of the Mexicans was accidentally hit in the neck by an arrow and killed. When his friends placed his body in front of the miraculous cloak, now mounted on the altar, he sat up.

Juan Diego went to live in a hut next to the shrine, where he became its curator and told the story of his visions to thousands of pilgrims from all over Mexico. He himself became known as 'The Pilgrim'.

By 1548, when both Juan Diego and Bishop Zumarraga died, 10 million Native Americans had converted to Christianity, moved by the story of the miraculous roses. In 1709 a great basilica was built near the foot of Tepeyac which attracted pilgrims from all over the world. In 1921 there was another miracle. Anti-Catholic militants planted a bomb on the altar at the basilica, close to the miraculous image. It exploded during Mass but no one was hurt and the image was not damaged.

Guadalupe was eventually swallowed up by the sprawling Mexico City. In 1976 a new Basilica of Our Lady of Guadelupe was built in the city, a huge round modernist structure in steel, wood, resinous fibres and polyethylene. In this astonishing structure you can glide past Juan Diego's cloak on a travelator! The basilica and its associated chapels constitute the most visited shrine to Our Lady in the western hemisphere with 12 million visitors every year. This, the latest of many shrines built on the site over the centuries, has a capacity of ten thousand.

A number of scientists have examined the cloak. Dr Philip Callahan of the US Department of Agriculture employed infrared techniques to date it and he verified its authenticity. Of course, it has been restored and embellished over the centuries, but the wonder of it is that, while the restorations and embellishments constantly fade, the original markings are as plain as ever.

Juan Diego was beatified by Pope John Paul II in 1990. His Feast Day is 9 December, the date of his original vision.

Information for Visitors

Location: Guadalupe is a town in central Mexico, 300 miles/482 km NW of Mexico City. **Contact Numbers:** TEL (52)5 521 7737. **Times of Services:** Sunday: 7.45 a.m., 11 a.m., 5 p.m. (Spanish); 9.30 a.m., 12.30 p.m., 7.30 p.m. (English); Saturday: 5.30 p.m.; Monday to Friday: 8 a.m. (Spanish); 5.30 p.m. (English).

— NETHERLANDS —

STAR OF THE SEA
MAASTRICHT

Hail thou Star of Ocean, Portal of the sky, Ever Virgin Mother Of the Lord Most High.
FROM THE EIGHTH-CENTURY HYMN *STELLA MARIS*

IT IS STRANGE to discover a shrine so far inland dedicated to Our Lady Stella Maris – Star of the Sea. The reason is that Maastricht stands on a strategically navigable river, the Meuse or Maas. Because of its position Maastricht has always been heavily defended and over the centuries has been the scene of many battles. The tenth-century cathedral is the most famous Marian shrine in the Netherlands and houses a relic traditionally accepted as a fragment of Our Lady's sash.

The cathedral also boasts a beautiful wooden statue of Our Lady, just over a metre high. She holds the Christ Child in one arm and in her other a vase containing a lily. This statue was brought to Maastricht in 1400 by a young nobleman, Nicholas von Harlaer, when he professed his vocation in the Franciscan Order. Nicholas lived to the grand age of 101 and is buried in front of the altar where the statue had been placed. There is an even more magnificent Madonna and Child, opulently jewelled and brocaded and dating from the fifteenth century, in the south aisle.

❖ THE LAME WALK

The statue presented by Nicholas has always been particularly venerated, especially by a solemn and sumptuous procession each Easter Monday. Tradition ascribes many miraculous cures to this Madonna and Child, none more meticulously investigated and authenticated than the case of Agnes Schryvers.

Little Agnes was deaf and dumb and crippled when her mother took her to see the Easter Monday procession in 1556. It was not customary in those days for children to attend the Eucharist, so Agnes's mother left the child in the Lady Chapel where she might look at the beautiful statue. At once Agnes stood up and began to talk for the first time in her life. She was in fact encouraging herself to walk, which she did – all the way from the Lady Chapel to the west door. This miraculous cure was one of many recorded by Friar Sedulius in a publication of 1609 which detailed all the healings in the church during his period of office there.

✤ A SKYLARK'S SONG

During the Thirty Years' War (1618–48) the statue was taken from the church and passed from house to house in order to save it from falling into the hands of the Calvinist soldiers who occupied Maastricht at the time. Throughout the religious wars of the sixteenth and seventeenth centuries the statue never had a settled home, and there are some delightful stories of its peripatetic career. For example, in the winter of 1633 the statue was lodged in a temporary shrine at Lichtenberg and tradition has it that a lark came out to sing daily around the plinth on which it was set. The great church was destroyed during these wars, but the Franciscans built a chapel in its ruins and placed the statue there in 1678.

After the restoration of the church in the nineteenth century, the tradition of Walking the Way of Our Lady strengthened. Often thousands of people would take part and the procession became the most frequent and populous witness to Our Lady in the Netherlands.

The Church of Our Lady Stella Maris is now designated a basilica and the statue is set in a chapel at the west end of the north aisle on the open porch, so that it can be seen from the street. There are few hours, day or night, when there is not a large group of pilgrims kneeling or standing in prayer before it.

Don't miss the Treasury Room which contains many treasures and objets d'art concerning the Blessed Virgin. The room itself is magnificently decorated.

On the Feast of the Assumption, 15 August, there is a very atmospheric candle-light procession.

For that fair blessed mother-maid,
Whose flesh redeemed us; that she-
    cherubin,
Which unlocked paradise, and made
One claim for innocence, and disseized sin,
Whose womb was a strange heaven, for
    there
God clothed himself, and grew,
Our zealous thanks we pour. As her deeds
    were
Our helps, so are her prayers; nor can she
    sue
In vain, who hath such titles unto you.

JOHN DONNE (1572–1631),
'THE VIRGIN MARY' FROM *A LITANY*

Information for Visitors

Location: near the Dutch–Belgian border. The shrine is located at Onze Lieve Vrouweplein 7. **Contact Number:** TEL (43) 325 1851. **Times of Services:** Sundays 9 a.m., 10 a.m., 11.30 a.m., 6 p.m.; Saturdays 9.30 a.m., 5 p.m., 6.30 p.m.; Monday-Friday 9.30 a.m.

— NEW ZEALAND —

STATUE OF MARY IMMACULATE
PARAPARAUMU

THE SHRINE TO MARY, MOTHER OF ALL
OTAKI

Hine Nui O Te Ao Katoa – (Mary, Great Woman of the Whole World).
MAORI DEDICATION

To mark the centenary of the appearances of Our Lady to St Bernadette at Lourdes (see p. 81) the parish priest of Paraparaumu, Father John Dunn, decided to build a large statue of the Blessed Virgin. The year was 1958 and the site chosen was the hill behind the parish church and school. The statue is modern in design and 14 metres tall. A marvellous sight from all the surrounding area, the figure of the Virgin is crowned with a halo and spectacularly illuminated at night.

The path leading up to the foot of the statue is marked by fourteen crosses in commemoration of Calvary and the Way of the Cross. Good Friday devotions include processions up this path and there is an annual pilgrimage to the statue, organised by the Legion of Mary, every February (on the Sunday closest to the 17th).

❖ WOMAN OF LIGHT

Not far from Paraparaumu is the coastal town of Otaki, and just inland is a hill on which grow karaka trees. The hill is called Pukekaraka in the Maori language. The whole area was entrusted to the Catholic Church by one of the local Maori tribes, the Ngati Kapu.

At the foot of Pukekaraka is a traditional meeting-place called a *marae*. This space and the house beside it are dedicated to *Hine Nui O Te Ao Katoa* (Mary, Great Woman of the Whole World, Woman of Light). It is a place where visitors are received and community business is conducted. The meeting-house features a large letter 'M' for Mary and a globe, topped by a Cross, representing the world. Another meeting-house has at its entrance the crossed keys that symbolize the custodianship of the Church given by Our

Lord Jesus Christ to St Peter and all his successors.

By the *marae* is a large stone wall known as the Wall of Reconciliation. People from the north of Otaki came and helped the locals build this wall in 1910 as a gesture of friendship, for previously the two communities had been enemies. Above and to the rear of the wall is a shrine to Mary, the Mother of All. It was built in 1901 and its grotto, modelled on that at Lourdes, dates from 1905. A path leading up the hill features the Stations of the Cross, and at the top is a Cross of iron.

Pukekaraka is also the site of ancient Maori graves, and the area at the top of the hill is used as a cemetery for deceased priests and sisters. A white cross marks the place where the first *raupo* (reed) church was built in 1844. Its first priest, Father Jean-Baptiste Compte of the Society of Mary, lived in a hut close by.

LEFT The statue of Our Lady at the shrine of Our Lady of Paraparaumu

Information for Visitors

Location: Paraparaumu and Otaki are about 45 miles/70 km N of Wellington, on the coast. **Contact Numbers:** TEL (4) 2985817 FAX (4) 2985817. **Times of Services:** Monday – Thursday: 9 a.m.; Friday: 11.15 a.m.; Saturday: 10 a.m. and Vigil Mass 7 p.m.; Sunday: Vigil Mass 10 a.m.

— POLAND —

THE BLACK MADONNA OF CZESTOCHOWA

I Jan Casimir, King of Poland, take thee as Queen and Patroness of my Kingdom. I place my people and my army under your protection.

JAN CASIMIR, 3 MAY 1656

ONE OF THE MOST charming of all the legends concerning Our Lady is the account of how, in fulfilment of her Son's dying words, she went to live at the house of St John, the beloved disciple. Tradition declares that she took with her a table which Jesus had made in the carpenter's workshop at Nazareth. Tradition again has it that St Luke painted the portrait of the Virgin on the table-top.

The painting was discovered in the fourth century by the same St Helen who was credited with finding Christ's Cross. Her son was the Emperor Constantine who decreed that the Roman Empire should be Christian; and it was Constantine who built a church in Constantinople to house St Luke's picture of Our Lady.

The portrait was kept there for hundreds of years, after which it was transported to Poland and came into the possession of Prince Ladislaus. The Prince kept the picture in his castle at Belz where, in the fourteenth century, an enemy arrow penetrated a high

window and lodged in the throat of the image.

Prince Ladislaus needed to find a safer resting-place for the holy picture and decided to take it to his birthplace, the city of Opala. On the way he rested at Czestochowa and stored the portrait overnight in the Church of the Assumption at the monastery of Jasna Gora. The next morning the picture was loaded on to the wagon again but the horses hitched to it refused to move. Prince Ladislaus saw this as a miraculous sign that the image of Our Lady should remain in Czestochowa. He built a church to display the picture, which remains there to this day.

In the Hussite wars of religion in the fifteenth century the church in Czestochowa was raided and its treasures stolen. The most valuable of these was the portrait. For the second time in its life it was placed on a wagon, and for the second time the horses refused to move. The Hussites, riled, threw the portrait down on the road. One of them slashed at it with his sword and mysteriously

Pope John Paul II has paid several visits to the National Shrine of Poland

collapsed and died in the very act of vandalism. Marks such as this that have been inflicted on the Virgin's picture have been painted over in the course of many attempted restorations, but have always strangely reappeared.

✤ THE MIRACLE AT THE VISTULA

At times of peril for the Polish nation the Virgin seems often to have lent support. In 1655 there was war between Sweden and Poland and, in thanksgiving for the Polish victory, the Virgin was acclaimed Queen of the Nation. On Holy Cross Day, 14 September 1920, a Russian army was camped by the River Vistula ready to invade Poland. Tradi-

tion says the enemy were deterred by a vision of Our Lady in the sky, and the episode is known as the Miracle at the Vistula. Pilgrimages were banned under the Nazi occupation during the Second World War and later under the Communists. Nevertheless millions risked their lives by paying public homage to Our Lady of Czestochowa.

✤ CZESTOCHOWA TODAY

The image of Our Lady has turned dark over the centuries through exposure to the elements and candle smoke, so that it is

OPPOSITE Our Lady of Czestochowa, also known as the Black Madonna

136

universally known as the Black Madonna. The picture has been the focus of many healing miracles and countless spiritual blessings, accounts of which are kept in the official records of the Pauline Monks at Jasna Gora.

The portrait of Our Lady of Czestochowa was crowned by Pope Clement XI in 1717 but the crown was stolen in 1909, only to be replaced by one even more glorious in gold and gemstones, the gift of Pope Pius X. Pope John Paul II, himself Polish, made a personal pilgrimage to the Black Madonna in 1979 and paid several more visits in the 1980s and 1990s. Czestochowa is the National Shrine of Poland, dedicated to its Patroness, the Queen of Heaven. The most important national Marian festival is on 3 May, when Our Lady is honoured in tremendous celebrations as Queen of Poland.

The chapel of the Blessed Virgin which houses the miraculous picture also features five other altars dedicated to major events in the life of the Holy Mother and of her Son, Jesus Christ. The altar piece which holds the picture is at the head of the chancel and next to it are placed the insignia of royal authority, the orb and sceptre set in gold and ornamented with precious stones. A golden rose brought to the shrine by Pope John Paul II is also displayed near the picture.

The haft of the royal sceptre is inscribed, 'Hail, Queen of the Polish crown! We Polish women offer this sceptre to you as the symbol of authority. Govern over us. Let the three evangelical virtues, Faith, Hope and Love lead thy people to glory.'

The orb is inscribed, 'Queen of the Polish crown, protect thy kingdom.'

Besides the 3 May celebrations, processions and many other elaborate decorations are held on all the feast days of Mary. There is the additional huge commemoration of Our Lady of Czestochowa on 26 August.

The shrine is opened daily at 5 a.m. and it closes at 9 p.m. The solemn devotions include the ceremony of the raising and lowering of the screen over the miraculous picture each day as follows:

raising 6 a.m. – lowering 12 noon
raising 3.30 p.m. – lowering 4.40 p.m.
raising 7 p.m. – lowering 7.45 p.m.
raising 9 p.m. – lowering 9.10 p.m.
(these times are susceptible to slight seasonal alteration).

Information for Visitors

Location: 120 miles/190 km SW of Warsaw.
Contact Numbers: TEL (34) 65 38 88 FAX (34) 65 43 43. **Times of Services:** Mass is said in front of the miraculous picture as follows: weekdays 6 a.m., 7 a.m., 7.30 a.m., 8 a.m. (Latin), 9.30 a.m., 11 a.m., 3.30 p.m. (4.45 p.m. and 5.30 p.m. most days), 6.30 p.m.; Sundays: as weekdays, with additional masses at 12 noon and 8.30 p.m.

THE VIRGIN OF FATIMA

O my Jesus, forgive us our sins, save us from the fires of hell, lead all souls to heaven, especially those in most need of your mercy.

TAUGHT BY OUR LADY OF FATIMA, 1917

IN THE EARLY twentieth century Portugal was in the midst of political upheaval and economic bankruptcy. It was an era of radical solutions. In 1911 the head of state, Alfonso Costa, promised to wipe out Catholicism 'within two generations'.

Fatima is a small village in the rocky central lowlands whose chief produce is olive oil. In 1916 nine-year-old Lucia Santos was sent by her parents to work as a shepherdess. One day that year she and her cousins Francisco Marto, aged eight, and his six-year-old sister Jacinta were out on the hillside when they saw a vision. 'It was a figure like a statue,' Lucia wrote many years later, 'made of snow that the rays from the sun had turned somewhat transparent.' She had other visions of this figure, 'a young man, about fourteen or fifteen years old, whiter than snow'. He said to them, 'Pray with me three times the prayer, "My God, I believe, I adore . . .".'

Later that year Lucia was playing by the well near her home with her cousins when the white angel again appeared and said, 'Pray, very much!' He told them that Jesus and Mary had plans for them.

✦ THE ANGEL'S PRAYER

Soon afterwards the three children were out in the countryside when the angel came to them once more and gave them a prayer which they must pray regularly:

Most Holy Trinity, Father, Son and Holy Ghost, I adore you profoundly. I offer you the most precious body, blood, soul and divinity of Jesus Christ, present in all the tabernacles of the world in reparation for the outrages, sacrileges and indulgences and indifferences by which he is offended. And through the infinite merits of the Sacred Heart of Jesus and the Immaculate Heart of Mary, I beg the conversion of poor sinners.

The angel held a chalice in his hand and the Host above it, both of which remained hanging in the air while he knelt to pray with the children.

Huge crowds gather in the courtyard in front of the basilica at Fatima

On 13 May 1917 Lucia, Jacinta and Francisco went out with their flock towards the valley of Cova da Iria. They saw two flashes of lightning and then 'a Lady, brighter than the sun' who said she was from heaven. Lucia – the only one of the three who ever spoke to the vision – asked, 'What do you want from me?'

The Lady replied, 'I want you to come here for six months in succession. Then I will tell you who I am and what I want.' She went on: 'Are you willing to offer yourselves to God and bear all the suffering he wills to send you, as an act of reparation for the sins by which he is offended and of prayer for the conversion of sinners?' On behalf of them all,

Lucia replied that they were indeed willing.

The Lady told them to pray the Rosary every day, for peace and the end of the war then raging elsewhere in Europe. She told them they would have much to suffer, then vanished in a brilliant light. The three friends agreed to say nothing to anyone, but in the late afternoon Jacinta met her parents and blurted out, 'Such a beautiful Lady!'

Keeping their promise, the children returned to Cova da Iria on 13 June at mid-day. About fifty people went with them. The Lady appeared again and told them that Francisco and Jacinta would soon be taken to heaven, but that Lucia would remain here on earth.

✧ THE DANCING SUN

On 13 July the children saw the vision again and Lucia, tired of the scepticism and ridicule of the villagers, asked her to perform a miracle as proof. The vision said she would do so on 13 October. She also showed them a vision of hellfire to which sinners must go. The Lady said, 'In order to prevent this, I come to ask for the consecration of Russia.' (1917 was, of course, the year of the atheistic Russian Revolution.) She went on, 'The Holy Father will consecrate Russia to me and it will be convert-ed, and a time of peace will be allowed for all the world.'

On 13 August the political authorities, irritated by the affair, took the children into custody and interrogated them separately, telling each of them that the others had been boiled in oil for their lies! But none of them recanted. When they were released, the Lady appeared and said she would keep her promise to perform the October miracle. She asked for a chapel to be built at Cova da Iria and for two trolleys to be constructed which might carry images of the Blessed Virgin in procession.

On 13 September thousands were present

Our Lady of Fatima

in the valley at midday but, although the Lady spoke with the children, the rest saw nothing. On 13 October an even greater crowd gathered. The day was dark and oppressive and, according to one newspaper report, 'far too misty to see visions'. It never stopped raining. But at noon precisely Lucia cried out, 'Silence! Our Lady is coming'. The vision told the children that a chapel should be built there in her honour. She said, 'I am the Lady of the Rosary. Pray the rosary every day. The war will end.' Then she ascended. There was a movement in the heavens, and thou-sands later described it in the words, 'The sun danced!'

Soon afterwards, Francisco fell seriously ill. Family and friends tried to reassure him, but he would only say, 'It's no use trying talking to me like that. Our Lady wants me in heaven.' Francisco was exceptionally devout and, throughout his long and painful illness, he always said, 'I want to try to comfort and console God for the offence that sinners have wrought against him.' Early on 4 April 1919 he called to his mother from his bedroom and asked if she could see a light in the doorway. He died at ten o'clock that morning.

Meanwhile, Jacinta expressed some disappointment that the Pope had not yet visited Fatima in response to the visions. This uneducated peasant child also said, 'The world is perishing because people will not pray.' She died of tuberculosis at the exact hour she had predicted: ten o'clock on the night of 20 February 1920. She was ten years old.

In 1921 the kindly Bishop of Fatima arranged for Lucia to be educated in Porto in the north, well away from the furore of Fatima. Eventually she became a Carmelite nun, taking the name Maria Lucia of the Immaculate Heart.

The first shrine at Fatima was built by a woman known as Maria da Capela, and consisted of a simple wooden arch and a Cross. This altar was dismembered by sceptics and paraded in mock procession through the streets. But word of the miraculous visions spread and soon there was an endless procession of pilgrims. The authorities thoroughly investigated the apparitions at Fatima and on 13 May 1930 declared that they were worthy of being attributed to supernatural causation. Gifts of money poured in from all over the world and the Vatican decided that, in order to avoid all hint of scandal or misappropriation, the money should be spent in Fatima itself. The result is one of the most impressive shrines to Our Lady in the world.

❖ THE SECRET OF FATIMA

Lucia wrote down the vision's words, which are known as the Secret of Fatima. Two parts of the message to the children have been widely published. The first was of the vision of hell given to the children on 13 July 1917: 'You have seen hell where the souls of poor sinners go. In order to save them, God wants you to establish in the world devotion to my Immaculate Heart. If you do as I say, many souls will be saved and there will be peace and the war will end. But if men do not cease offending God, another and more terrible war will break out!' The second part of the Secret was that devotion should be established worldwide to the Immaculate Heart of Mary.

The third part of the Secret was read by Pope John XXIII in 1960 and Pope Paul VI in 1963, but never publicly revealed. Veiled references in papal preachings suggest promises that the Catholic faith will never be extinguished in Portugal, that Russia would one day soon be converted and so glorify God, and that all Christians will eventually be made one according to Christ's prayer before his Passion and Crucifixion.

In 1997 there were earthquakes in Italy and some people feared they might be precursors of apocalyptic disturbances. Senior members of the Sacred Congregation in Rome spoke out to quell rumours that the third part of the Fatima Secret refers to the end of the world.

❖ FATIMA TODAY

The shrine adjoins the village and completely dominates it. There are huge terraces in stone and concrete, and an impressive pilgrims' way descends from the hills to the south into the centre of the courtyard of the basilica. Penitents can be seen at all times approaching along this way, many on their hands and knees.

Don't miss the little Chapel of the Apparitions in the heart of the sanctuary, built by local people in 1919 in fulfilment of Our Lady's request. The large holm oak beneath which the visionaries awaited the coming of the Virgin is still there. The Hostel of Our Lady of Dolours to the left of the sanctuary receives the sick on large pilgrimage days. There is also a Perpetual Adoration Chapel with a permanent exhibition of the Blessed Sacrament.

The tower of the basilica is some 65 metres tall, surmounted by a cross of bronze weighing seven tonnes and a great crystal cross which is lit up during the evening services. The painting over the high altar depicts the descent of Our Lady to the children. The remains of Francisco and Jacinta are interred inside the basilica. At nearby Valinhos, where Our Lady appeared for the fourth time, there is a commemorative shrine in the form of a statue of the Virgin beneath an arch.

On 12 May 1982 Pope John Paul II made a pilgrimage to Fatima and gave thanks to Our Lady for saving his life after he had been shot the previous year. He celebrated Mass at the shrine and gave Holy Communion to Sister Lucia, the sole surviving member of the original band of visionaries.

Pilgrims flock to Fatima all year round and often the little country lanes are congested with coaches and cars approaching from every direction. The 13th of each month is a day of special processions and on 13 May each year half a million pilgrims attend the anniversary commemorations.

Each pilgrimage involves the following devotions:
- the praying of the Rosary
- the candlelight procession
- Mass
- annointing of the sick
- the Adeus procession in which thousands of pilgrims wave white handkerchiefs in a gesture of farewell to the statue of Our Lady.

Cova da Iria, the place of one of the visions, is now in the shrine grounds and here is the Chapel of Apparitions, the basilica where Francisco and Jacinta's mortal remains are interred and the chapel of Perpetual Adoration. Here also is the holm oak tree.

The homes of the visionaries are about twenty minutes' walk from the Cova da Iria.

Information for Visitors

Location: about 70 miles/110 km NE of Lisbon. **Contact Numbers:** TEL (49) 530 1000 FAX (49) 530 1005 INTERNET: www.fatima.org. **Times of Services:** throughout the day including Mass, Rosary and Prayer of Reparation to the Immaculate Heart of Mary. In English: July–September 3.30 p.m. in the Capelinha, 4–6 p.m. Confessions. **Special Events:** Pilgrimages on 12th and 13th of month.

THE GATHERING OF THE DISPLACED
KIBEHO

This world is on the edge of catastrophe.
OUR LADY TO MARIE-CLAIRE MUKANGANGO, 20 MARCH 1982

ALPHONSINE MUMUREKE, aged sixteen, was a pupil at Kibeho College, a religious foundation run by the Benebikira Sisters. She was serving at table on 28 November 1981 when she heard a voice call out to her, 'My daughter.' Startled, she looked about her but she could not identify the speaker. She went on her way, out of the dining room and into the long corridor. Suddenly before her was the vision of a beautiful young woman, all in white. Alphonsine instinctively fell to her knees and asked the woman who she was.

The apparition replied in the local Kinyarwanda language, '*Nai Nyrina wa Jambo,*' meaning 'I am the Mother of the Word.' The Word is, of course, the title which St John gives to Jesus in his Gospel, and is the translation of an expression in Greek philosophy which signifies the rational or organizing principle by which the world was created. Alphonsine's vision declared herself to be the Mother of the Word, the Blessed Virgin Mary.

✦ BE A LITTLE CHILD WITH ME

The Virgin asked Alphonsine what she understood of religion. The girl replied instantly, like one trained to repeat the catechism: 'I love God and His Mother who has given us the gift of their Son, Jesus. It is Jesus who saves us.'

Our Lady smiled her approval and said, 'I wish some of your companions had as much faith!' And she told Alphonsine that she wanted her to join the Legion of Mary, a missionary society supervised by the Catholic bishops of Rwanda. Then the Virgin arose slowly into the air and disappeared from sight.

The girl collapsed and fell into a trance from which she was roused only with great difficulty by one of the teachers. Alphonsine had been babbling and the teacher wondered if she was ill. On hearing her story, everyone at the college told her not to be such a fool. On 29 November, Advent Sunday, Alphonsine received a second vision. Our Lady was most anxious to convince the girl of her tender, motherly nature: 'I love children who will play with me, because this shows their love and trust. Be as a little child with me, for I love to pet you.' Again Alphonsine's teacher and friends made fun of her. Because of this widespread mockery one of Alphonsine's closest friends prayed that the Virgin would manifest herself to another pupil so that there might be confirmation of her testimony.

On 12 January 1982 the Blessed Virgin appeared to sixteen-year-old Anathalie Mukamazimpaka, a member of the Legion of Mary. Anathalie's messages were deeply theological and spiritual. Our Lady told her that she was to command her friends and teachers: 'Wake up and stand upright. Purify yourselves and contemplate. Give yourselves to continual prayer. Be charitable and humble.' The evidence of this second visionary began to convince the school that they had indeed received a visitation from the mother of the Word.

On 22 March Our Lady appeared to twenty-two-year-old Marie-Claire Mukangango, another pupil at Kibeho. She told her friends, 'We are to pray the passion of the Lord Jesus Christ and of his Mother who stood by the Cross, weeping. We must say the Rosary and pray for forgiveness.' Our Lady instructed Marie-Claire to pray the Beads of the Seven Sorrows.

News of the apparitions and messages spread and many people travelled to Kibeho to investigate their meaning. Alphonsine, Vestine and Anathalie also experienced extended trances in which Our Lady accompanied them on a visionary tour of heaven, hell and purgatory. While the young people were in these trance states they could not be moved or lifted from where they lay. Alphonsine even warned her Mother Superior about these events: 'From 20 March do not try to lift me for two days. I will be as one who is dead. But I pray, do not bury me.' The nuns and teachers built wooden platforms so that visitors could observe the girls in these visionary trances.

Sometimes the visionaries would dance ecstatically. Always they insisted that the Virgin's messages were for the whole world. The crowds who witnessed these happenings also saw wonders in the sky – the sun spinning as it had done at Fatima (see p. 141), and sometimes two or more suns in the heavens, crosses and crowns of thorns emblazoned on the clouds. Agnes warned that the end of the world was near and that people must prepare for it.

✤ TRUE LOVE COMES FROM GOD

Beyond the school, the Virgin appeared also to twenty-two-year-old Agnes Kamagaju in her own house on 2 June. She announced herself as 'Mother of Heaven' and 'The Immaculate Conception', just as she had done to St Bernadette at Lourdes. On 18 August Agnes received a vision of Jesus, who said, 'Young people should not use their bodies as instruments of pleasure. True love comes from God. Do not put yourselves at the service of money. Pray to Mary, your Mother.'

Around this time, Jesus appeared also to fifteen-year-old Emmanuel Segatashya while he was gathering crops in his father's field. Emmanuel had no religious training and his vision of Christ taught him to say the Lord's

Prayer. People were very sceptical when they heard of Emmanuel's vision – he was, after all, only an ignorant peasant boy. But Emmanuel addressed a curious crowd of over three thousand people: 'If I have not been sent by Jesus, of whom before I knew nothing, then who could possibly have sent me?'

The boy, who did not even know the meaning of the Cross, began to criticize the clergy for their laxity: 'You do not take sufficient care of those who are physically and spiritually weak. You think too much of money. And you have neglected your vow of chastity.' Emmanuel also announced that the Day of Judgement and the end of the world were very near.

The most unlikely of all the Rwandan visionaries was twenty-four-year-old Vestine Salina, for she was a Muslim. The Virgin told Vestine that she must become a shepherdess and lead her neighbours back to God. Vestine was often seen carrying a shepherd's staff. All the visionaries joined in a corporate fast for the forty days of Lent in 1983.

✤ AN AWFUL PROPHECY

One of the most disturbing of the visions given to the young people was of a river of blood in which hordes of Rwandans killed one another indiscriminately. This was a terribly accurate prophecy of the coming war between the Hutus and the Tutsis in which millions perished.

Bishop Jean-Baptiste Gahamagi issued a pastoral encyclical on 30 July 1983 in which he said, 'There should be no surprise if the Church expresses its judgement only after a fairly long period. Many years are often required for the truth to emerge. We ask, therefore, that you be patient.'

The last apparition at Kibeho took place on 28 November 1989, exactly eight years after the first, with a crowd of twelve thousand who had come together at Alphonsine's request. Just after midday she told the assembly that she was seeing the Holy Mother again. Our Lady asked her for a church to be built in Kibeho, to be dedicated to the Gathering of the Displaced. She asked that it should be a place where the prayer 'Maranatha' – Come, O Lord and redeem thy people – should be sung constantly. It has become a place of international pilgrimage.

The main pilgrim services are held on all the major festivals of Our Lady. Ceremonies on 28 November commemorate Alphonsine's original vision.

Information for Visitors

Location: 190 miles/305 km from Kigali.
Contact Numbers: (*Butare Diocese Head Office*) TEL 30327 FAX 30066. **Times of Services:** weekdays 6.30 a.m., Sundays 7.30 a.m. and 10 a.m., 1st Saturday in month 8 a.m. (Pilgrims), 25 March, 15 August, 15 September and 28 November 11 a.m. (Pilgrims).

OUR LADY OF HADDINGTON

EAST LOTHIAN

While we sang, all the clergy moved among us, reaching out to the lame, the disabled and the distressed. So powerful is the emotion that it is hardly surprising to hear accounts of remarkable recoveries.

LADY OLGA MAITLAND

IN THE TWELFTH century there was a stone statue of the Infant Jesus in his Mother's arms in the church at Whitekirk, near Haddington on the east coast. Famous all over Europe, it was known as Our Lady of Haddington. The shrine was very popular among pilgrims in the Middle Ages, and many thousands visited every year to pay homage to the Virgin and say their prayers.

In 1435 Aeneas Sylvius Piccolomini, a papal emissary, was sent on a diplomatic mission to the Scottish court. After a stormy North Sea crossing in which he and his entourage were nearly shipwrecked, he was anxious to give thanks for his safe arrival. Piccolomini made for the shrine at Whitekirk, only to find that it had been vandalized by the English in one of the many border skirmishes of the times. He wrote in his memoirs: 'All the monks had deserted the holy place. There wasn't even any food there, and so we had to go to the next village.'

❖ THE LAMP OF LOTHIAN

This village was Haddington, where the inhabitants were building a grand new church dedicated to the Blessed Virgin Mary. The remains of the despoiled shrine at Whitekirk were transported to Haddington and re-established as the Altarage of the Blessed Virgin and the Three Kings in about 1450. As a place of renowned spiritual illumination, St Mary's Haddington has became known as the Lamp of Lothian.

In 1547–8 Haddington was besieged by an English army and St Mary's Church was all but destroyed. In 1561 the reformer John Knox suggested that the church be repaired, but the town council was short of funds and could only restore the building 'frae the steeple to the west end'. For 410 years the devastated church stood roofless and open to the elements. At last in 1971 a full restoration was begun.

The stone representation of the Madonna and Child

The entrance to the shrine showing the Burning Bush, commonly used as the Presbyterian Church symbol in Scotland but also regarded as the symbol of Our Lady's perpetual virginity

RUBUM INCOMBUSTUM CONSERVATEM AGNOVIMUS TUAM LAUDIBILEM VIRGINI- TATEM DEI GENE- TRIX INTERCEDE PRO NOBIS

❖ KINGS IN KILTS

At about that time, the new 17th Earl of Lauderdale discovered that his title made him custodian of part of St Mary's Church known as the Lauderdale Aisle. He decided to turn the Lauderdale Aisle into an ecumenical chapel and to restore the ancient Altar of the Blessed Virgin and the Three Kings.

Information for Visitors

Location: on A1 about 15 miles/25 km E of Edinburgh. St Mary's Church is open Monday–Saturday, 10 a.m.–4 p.m., April to end of September. **Contact Number:** TEL (01620) 823019. **Times of Services:** Sundays 9.30 a.m. (family service), 11 a.m. (parish communion). Open to visitors 1–4 p.m.

He commissioned Anton Wagner, a native of Oberammergau, to make new carvings for the shrine, including the famous Three Kings in Kilts. This is not so eccentric as it might appear: in Aberdeen there is a fifteenth-century Adoration of the Magi in which the Kings wear the kilt. The Fifteen Mysteries of the Holy Rosary are embroidered on mats in the Three Kings chapel, and there is a carved stone representation of the Madonna and Child.

❖ THE ANNUAL PILGRIMAGE

The highlight of the year at Haddington is the annual pilgrimage on the second Saturday in May. This is a truly ecumenical occasion when priests, ministers and congregations from the Orthodox, Anglican, Roman Catholic and Presbyterian Churches gather for a united service of prayers, thanksgiving and healing. Testimonies from people who have received blessing and relief from their illnesses now run into many thousands.

MARY, TABERNACLE OF THE MOST HIGH
NGOME

*Mary showed herself in a wonderful light, more beautiful than the sun. She was robed
all in white, flowing veil from top to toe. Upon her breast rested a big Host surrounded by a
brilliant corona, radiating life.*

SISTER REINOLDA MAY, 22 AUGUST 1955

SISTER REINOLDA MAY was born in 1901
in Pfalzheim, Germany, into a farming
family. Under the influence of her parish
priest, she discovered her vocation and joined
the Benedictine Sisters of Tutzing. In 1925
she went to work as a medical missionary in
what was then Zululand.

In 1955 she began to receive visions of the
Virgin. The first happened in August in the
chapel where Reinolda had just received
Communion. She described the experience as
'like entering a cloud, drawn by Mary away
from the earth. I was very much dazzled by
the beauty and the light I had seen.'

Our Lady spoke to her out of the radiance:
'Call me Tabernacle of the Most High. You
too are such a tabernacle. Believe it. I wish to
be called upon by this title for the glory of my
Son. I wish that more such tabernacles be
prepared. I wish that altars be surrounded by
praying people more frequently. Do not be
afraid, make it known.'

Further visions followed in October and
then, in March 1956, the Virgin appeared
again after Mass and said, 'My child, I know
about your anxiety. You asked for a sign?'
Reinolda replied that she wanted one only to
satisfy sceptics. Our Lady answered: 'I wish
that a shrine be erected for me in the place
where seven springs came together. There I
let my graces flow in abundance. Many
people shall turn to God.' When Reinolda
asked where the place of seven springs was,
the Virgin only made a pointing movement.

After various further appearances the
Virgin spoke to Reinolda with great urgency
in April 1958.

'Only a flaming sea of hosts can drive back
the hate of the godless world and restrain the
angry hand of the Father.' This time when
Reinolda asked again about the place of the
springs the Virgin answered, 'On your
property on the mountain.'

Reinolda's claims met with mixed

responses. Some of her colleagues dismissed her testimony but others believed, including Father Ignatius Jutz, the Superior of the Nongoma Mission and Secretary General of the Benedictine hospitals. The local Bishop was cautious but did consent to the building of a shrine at Ngome, the place where seven springs flowed together. It was blessed by Father Ignatius on Whitsunday 1966.

Reinolda received two further apparitions of the Blessed Virgin: on 23 March 1970, after she had suffered a terrible vision of the Devil in the night, and on 2 May 1971, in the hospital chapel, where a picture of Our Lady appeared suddenly to be full of her life and presence. In 1980 Reinolda fell ill and moved to nearby Inkamana. She died at the Abbey there on 1 April 1981 and is buried in the Abbey cemetery.

✤ A PLACE OF PRAYER

In August 1985 Bishop Mansuet Biyase blessed a larger chapel which had been built on a rock opposite the first little shrine. A picture of Our Lady, Tabernacle of the Most High, painted, according to Reinolda's description, by a German artist, was placed in the new shrine. In October 1992 Bishop Biyase blessed an open-air altar at the shrine

and declared that it should be officially reverenced as 'a place of prayer'. In 1977 the Benedictine Sisters of Twasana set up a Community of Adoration at the shrine. Saturday has been appointed as the main day for pilgrimages after each of the major festivals of Our Lady, chiefly the Annunciation, Mother and Queen, Immaculate Conception and Holy Rosary.

Information for Visitors

Location: on the edge of Teas Estate in Natal, 50 miles/80 km outside Vryheid on road to Nongoma. Accommodation for pilgrims at Inkamana Abbey. **Contact Numbers:** TEL (381) 812 577 FAX (381) 809 689. **Times of Services:** daily Mass 6 a.m., 11.45 a.m. Midday Prayers, 5.30 p.m. Vespers, Sunday Mass 7.30 a.m. and 10 a.m. **Special Events:** pilgrimages on Saturday after 25 March (Annunciation), 22 August (Mother and Queen), 8 December (Immaculate Conception), first Saturday in October (Holy Rosary) and 1 May.

OUR LADY OF MOUNT CARMEL

GARABANDAL

Ask us sincerely and we will give to you. You should sacrifice more. Think of the Passion of Jesus.
THE HOLY MOTHER TO THE CHILDREN AT GARABANDAL, 19 JUNE 1965

ON SUNDAY, 18 June 1961, four girls were returning from Mass in the village of San Sebastian in the Cantabrian mountains. Their names were Mari Loli Mazon, Jacinta Gonzalez, Maria Cruz Gonzalez and Conchita Gonzalez. Maria Cruz was eleven and the others twelve. They picked some apples from a little orchard on the hillside without asking the owner's permission, and afterwards felt guilty. They sat on the stony path, looking glum.

Suddenly they saw a tall, silent figure in white, surrounded by a brilliant light, in the form of a winged angel. When the girls ran home and told their family and friends, they were laughed at. Next day they went back up the hill in the hope of seeing the figure again, but it did not appear.

✦ WE SHALL BE PUNISHED

The following Wednesday the girls decided to return to the site and pray. This time they went accompanied by friends. The silent angel appeared to the four girls as they knelt and smiled at them, but the bystanders saw nothing. The vision was repeated six days running. More and more villagers accompanied the visionaries, some in hope, some out of idle curiosity and others to mock the girls' credulity.

On 1 July the angel spoke for the first time and told the children that the following day they would see the Blessed Virgin as Our Lady of Mount Carmel, the hill in Israel associated with the prophet Elijah.

Next day she duly appeared, accompanied by two angels, in the area known as the Pines at Garabandal. The Virgin continued to appear throughout that month. Each time the girls went into ecstasy, during which they exhibited extraordinary physical changes: they became insensitive to pinpricks, extreme noise and bright lights, and their slight bodies could hardly be lifted from the ground by two strong men.

The two thousand or so appearances at Garabandal between 1961 and 1965 are among the most charming and yet the most terrifying of all the apparitions of Our Lady. Conchita described how the Virgin would pass the Infant Jesus to one of the girls to cuddle, or remove her crown and let the girls try it on. But she also issued some terrible warnings. On 4 July 1961 she said, 'Many sacrifices must be made. Much penance must be done. We must pay many visits to the Blessed Sacrament. Above all, we must be very good. If we do not do these things, then punishment awaits us. Already the cup is filling and if we do not change our ways we shall be punished.'

✤ OUT-OF-BODY EXPERIENCES

The Holy Mother followed her dreadful warnings with the announcement of a great miracle to occur among the pines at Garabandal. It would be a permanent sign and might be photographed, though no one would be allowed to touch it. Our Lady also prophesied that there would be only three Popes after John XXIII 'until the end of time'.

The girls received out-of-body experiences during which they claimed they were taken on spiritual journeys through the heavens by the Virgin. Many eyewitnesses declared on oath that they had observed the girls seeming to fly over the ground at great speed when Our Lady was calling them to her.

The girls were subjected to rigorous interrogation by the Church authorities and, confused, withdrew their claims. These retractions should not be treated too seriously, however, as they were obtained under great duress. Besides, there were many independent eyewitnesses who were convinced that the events at Garabandal were of supernatural origin.

✤ MIRACULOUS COMMUNION

One of these events is perhaps the most sensational in the whole history of Our Lady's appearances. On 22 June 1962, the Archangel Michael promised Conchita the Miracle of the Visible Communion – she would receive the Blessed Sacrament without any priest to administer it. At 1 a.m. on 19 July 1962, Conchita indeed received the Host from an invisible hand. Many saw it suddenly appear on her tongue, and there is even a photograph of the event.

In August 1961 the diocesan bishop urged Catholics to ignore the events at Garabandal, and forbade visiting priests to say Mass in the parish church. This ban was lifted by his successor in 1987. There has been no official pronouncement declaring the validity of the apparitions at Garabandal, but neither have they been condemned.

Conchita emigrated to New York in 1972, worked as a nurse, married and had four children. In 1980 she helped make a BBC film in which she affirmed the reality of the visions.

✤ THE SHRINE TODAY

Garabandal is one of the most dramatic and controversial of all the claimed apparitions of Our Lady, yet it still awaits official authentication. Even so, thousands of pilgrims visit the little mountain village every year and pray to the Virgin.

The Rosary is said every evening but the time varies according to the hours of daylight. In January this service is at 6.00 p.m., and the time advances by half-hour stages as we move into spring and summer.

On 18 June there is a commemoration among the pines of the vision of St Michael.

Every day in November there are prayers at 6.00 a.m. for souls in purgatory. The village maintains the ancient custom of arranging for a bell-ringer to walk about through the narrow streets and call the people to pray for those in purgatory.

Information for Visitors

Location: about 57 miles/96 km SE of Santander near the Picos de Europa mountains on N coast. **Contact Number:** TEL (42) 72 71 13 or call St Michael's Garabandal Centre in the US on (818) 3033 or e-mail j-tip@ix.netcom.com **Times of Services:** weekdays 10 a.m. (except Tuesday and Friday), Tuesdays and Fridays 9 a.m., Sundays 1.15 p.m.

LA MORENETA
MONTSERRAT

In all ages, the sinful, the suffering and the sorrowful have laid their troubles at the feet of Our Lady of Montserrat and none has ever gone away unheard or unaided.

ANONYMOUS TWENTIETH-CENTURY ARCHIVIST OF MONTSERRAT

THE PEOPLE OF north-eastern Spain are a proud and independent race and you will often hear the expression, only half in jest, 'We have nothing to do with Madrid!' This is Catalonia, an ancient province with its own language and local customs.

Montserrat is a mountain in the foothills of the Pyrenees, and the name means 'Sawn Mountain' on account of its jagged peaks. Halfway up stands the church, which is home to a miraculous wooden statue of the Madonna and Child.

The crowned Virgin wears a plain dress and cape and holds in her right hand a globe. The Infant Jesus, in kingly apparel and with his hand raised in benediction, sits on his

The spectacular setting of the shrine in the foothills of the Pyrenees

Mother's knee. This famous statue is called La Moreneta, meaning Dark Little One, and is officially listed as a Black Madonna (see p. 27).

This beautiful, tender image was originally called La Jerosolimitana because legend said it was carved in Jerusalem in the earliest days of the Christian Church. It is said to have connections with St James, who was leader of the Church in Jerusalem and whose own shrine is at Santiago da Compostela in the north of Spain. Somehow the statue was given into the keeping of St Eteres, Bishop of Barcelona, who is credited with bringing it to Spain.

✤ MYSTERIOUS SINGING

In the eighth century Spain was invaded by the Moors and Barcelona was besieged for more than three years. In 718, on the edge of defeat, the people of the city moved the statue to a cave on Montserrat. In 890 two young

shepherds discovered the statue after hearing mysterious singing coming from the cave. They sent for the priest and the priest alerted the bishop. Shepherds, priest and bishop all heard the singing and saw bright lights over the mountain.

Soon plans were put in hand for the building of a church, though the one which now stands on the spot was built in 1592. The statue stands high in an alcove over the main altar and can be reached by stairs to a room behind the alcove which is known as the Virgin's Chamber. Here pilgrims offer their devotion to Our Lady.

A Benedictine monastery was built next to the church, and both buildings have been attacked and damaged by invading armies. They were first despoiled in the Napoleonic Wars in the early nineteenth century and again in sporadic revolutionary uprisings in the following hundred years. Mercifully the statue remained undamaged, even during the Civil War of 1936–9.

Pope Leo XIII (1878–1903) declared Our Lady of Montserrat to be Patroness of the Diocese of Catalonia.

OPPOSITE The wooden statue of La Moreneta, or 'Dark Little One', which is said to have been carved in Jerusalem in the earliest days of the Christian Church

✤ VISITING THE SHRINE

Each year more than a million pilgrims visit the shrine, which is one of the most popular holy places in Spain.

Here is the oldest boys' choir in Europe and they sing the *Salve Regina* at 1.00 p.m. and a motet after 6.45 p.m. Vespers every day.

The monks invite pilgrims to join in all the daily offices and the Liturgy of the Hours. Don't miss the chance to visit the cave where the original statue was found.

The mountain has been declared a nature park and is a favourite place for pleasant walks to spectacular vantage points including *The Fra Gari* vantage point, *The Cross of Saint Michael, Sant Jeroni and Sant Joan* (which can also be reached by cable car). The nearby Museum of Montserrat houses a display of paintings, sculptures, drawings, engravings and medals which show how the artistic representation of Our Lady of Montserrat has changed through the ages. It also contains archaeological items from the Bible lands, gold and silver liturgical items, classical paintings and modern paintings and sculpture.

Information for Visitors

Location: about 20 miles/32 km NW of Barcelona. **Contact Numbers:** TEL (38) 35 02 51 FAX (38) 28 40 49. **Times of Services:** Basilica, daily, 11 a.m. Vespers 6.45 p.m.

SWITZERLAND

OUR LADY OF EINSIEDELN

Stop! For this church has been divinely consecrated.

THE HEAVENLY VOICE TO BISHOP CONRAD AT THE DEDICATION OF THE CHURCH AT EINSIEDELN IN AD 948

MEINRAD WAS a ninth-century Benedictine monk at the monastery of Reichenau who in 840 realized that he had a vocation to the solitary life. He received permission to live as a hermit in a secluded hollow on Mount Etzel. He became an object of curiosity and was often disturbed by staring crowds, so he made a new hermitage for himself among the pines by Lake Lucerne.

Even there, a brother monk from Reichenau begged to be allowed to call on him. One evening this visitor was approaching the hermitage when he saw the whole place surrounded by a brilliant light. He looked through the window and saw Meinrad at his prayers, the book held open by a supernatural child who was reciting the verses with him. Meinrad's visitor spread the news that the former Reichenau monk entertained angels.

Alone in the forest, Meinrad developed a deep relationship with its creatures and had two tame crows as pets. His reputation as a man with outstanding spiritual gifts spread, and he was forever being called upon for

counsel. It seemed right that these pilgrims and visitors to the hermitage should hear Mass, and for this purpose a little chapel was built there in 853.

The chapel was provided by the Abbess Hildegarde of Zurich, who also presented Meinrad with a beautiful wooden statue of Our Lady. Pilgrims began to report cures after visiting Meinrad's chapel, which was now dedicated to Our Lady of Einsiedeln.

❖ THE MURDER OF MEINRAD

On a winter night in 863 Meinrad received a vision in which he was told that he would be set upon by two thieves who would murder him. Soon afterwards the robbers arrived, anticipating rich pickings from the money and jewels left at the shrine by grateful pilgrims. Despite knowing their evil intent, Meinrad welcomed them and gave them food and drink.

Then they ransacked the chapel, found nothing worth stealing, and in their fury set upon Meinrad and beat him to death. They placed his body on the bed so that anyone arriving in the early morning would think the hermit was only asleep, giving them more time to escape. As they lifted the monk's body, two nearby candles suddenly burst into light. The terrified killers ran off into the forest. What they could not know was that Meinrad's pet crows had followed them all the way to Zurich.

A woodcutter who knew Meinrad well heard cawing in the darkness and realized that something must be wrong. He ran to the hermitage and discovered the body of his friend. Meinrad's funeral was held at Reichenau Abbey, and he was mourned by thousands throughout that part of Switzerland.

✤ TWO FAITHFUL CROWS

The murderers were brought to justice and legend has it that Meinrad's crows flew over the scaffold at their execution. This is the explanation for the statues and pictures of crows found in Swiss churches. Crows became the emblem of Einsiedeln Abbey, and there are inns and retreats around Zurich named Two Faithful Crows.

Sadly, Meinrad's chapel fell into disrepair. But in 903 it was visited by a canon named Benno from Strasbourg, who restored it and founded a small community of Benedictine monks there. He built a church to house the little chapel and to preserve it as a shrine to the memory of Meinrad. The building was finished in 948 and its consecration set for Holy Cross Day.

The ceremony was to be performed by Conrad, Bishop of Constance, who spent the previous night kneeling in vigil before the statue of Our Lady in Meinrad's chapel. There he received a vision of an angelic choir singing the consecration anthems. At the head of the angels, standing before the altar, was Our Lord, preparing to conduct the solemn rite of consecration. In this heavenly company were also St Stephen, St Augustine, St Peter, St Gregory and St Lawrence. On a separate throne in the sanctuary sat the Blessed Virgin.

Bishop Conrad noticed that they slightly altered the words of the *Benedictus Qui Venit* to 'Blessed be the Son of Mary, who has descended to this place; who liveth and reigneth, world without end. Amen.'

At dawn when monks and attendants arrived, he told them the consecration had already taken place. The priests convinced him, however, that the service should go ahead as planned. But when the opening sentences were being intoned a heavenly voice commanded: 'Stop! For this church has been divinely consecrated.'

✤ THE DARK FOREST

Bishop Conrad later wrote all this down and offered his account to Pope Leo VIII. In 964, the Holy Father officially confirmed the miracle of the divine consecration. Bishop Conrad's book *De Secretis Secretorum* can be seen in the abbey at Einsiedeln.

The church was burnt down in 1028 but the inner chapel of Meinrad was spared. At the same time, Meinrad was consecrated by Pope Benedict IX and his bones brought back to Einsiedeln where he had been murdered.

Five churches on the site were destroyed by fire, but each time the chapel of St Meinrad was unharmed. After the fifth fire in 1577, the building was reconstructed in stone and marble.

In 1791 the church was plundered by French revolutionary forces, but the statue of Our Lady was saved because a monk concealed it in the bottom of a tinker's satchel. The statue was returned to the shrine in 1803.

The statue of Our Lady is simply breath taking – a majestic black figure dressed and crowned in gold and holding on her left arm the Infant Jesus. Since 1600 she has been clothed in the style of the Spanish court.

The spectacular church, its west side some 446 feet/136 metres in length, has symmetrical twin towers with citron-shaped cupolas. It nestles beneath the hillside in countryside known as the Dark Forest, and looks magnificent when illuminated at night. The interior is dazzlingly ornate in baroque white and gold. Look upwards to the Christmas Cupola, an enchanting eighteenth-century fresco of the manger scene by Cosmas Damien Asam. The Chapel of Meinrad, restored and rebuilt, is in the middle of the church on what is believed to be its original location.

Every year the shrine attracts 200,000 pilgrims from all over the world. Each 21 January, a Pontifical High Mass is said in commemoration of Meinrad and on this day the relic of the saint's head is venerated in the Lady Chapel. The Feast of Our Lady of Einsiedeln is celebrated on the Sunday following 16 July with High Mass and Solemn Procession after Vespers. On 15 August, the Feast of the Assumption, there is a Pontifical High Mass. (Over the high altar there is a magnificent painting by Franz Kraus representing the Assumption of Our Lady.) There are elaborate ceremonies commemorating all the festivals of Our Lady. The pilgrimage season ends on Rosary Sunday at the beginning of October. But on 8 December, the Immaculate Conception, there is an annual pilgrimage on foot, through the long hours of an often icy night, by the Catholic academics and students from Zurich to Our Lady of Hermits in whose shrine they celebrate Mass in the darkness of early morning.

Information for Visitors

Location: S of Zurich and E of Lucerne. **Contact Numbers:** TEL (55) 418 61 11 FAX (55) 418 62 30 or (55) 418 61 12. **Times of Services:** from Easter to All Hallows: weekdays 8.30 a.m., 11 a.m. and 5 : 30 p.m. Mass in Mercy Chapel. Sundays and feast days 8 a.m. parish worship, 9 : 30 a.m. High Mass, 11 a.m. parish worship, 5.30 p.m. Mass (High Altar), 7.25 p.m. Rosary. 1 November – Easter: weekdays 9.30 a.m. and 5.30 p.m. Mass (Unterkirche), 7.25 p.m. Rosary (Unterkirche). Sundays and feast days 8.30 a.m. parish worship, 9.30 a.m. High Mass, 11 a.m. parish worship, 5.30 p.m. Mass (Jugendkirche), 7.25 p.m. Rosary (Unterkirche).

OUR LADY OF DAMASCUS

God saves me.
Jesus enlightens me.
The Holy Spirit is my life.
Therefore I shall not fear.

PRAYER TAUGHT BY OUR LADY TO MYRNA NAZZOUR, 18 DECEMBER 1982

OUR LADY DOES not always appear only to people who have a well-developed religious sense. Nicholas and Maria Nazzour, for example, were nominal Greek Orthodox Christians living in Damascus. They were married when Maria, known as Myrna, was only eighteen and, like most young couples, they enjoyed the night-life of the city.

In November 1982, Nicholas's sister Layla fell seriously ill. Myrna felt a strong desire to pray for her, and her hands suddenly began to ooze oil. She was astonished, but two other women praying with her said, 'It's oil for healing. Place your hands on Layla!' She did so, and Layla instantly recovered. A few days later, a small statue of the Madonna and Child in Myrna's bedroom also began to ooze oil.

Nicholas gathered his whole family and they knelt in prayer, asking God to explain these strange events. As they prayed, oil oozed from a household icon – enough to fill several small dishes. Although the family were praying aloud, Myrna could not hear them. It

was as if she had fallen into a trance and was temporarily deaf. Later she testified to hearing an inner voice saying, 'Myrna, don't be afraid. I am with you. Open the doors and do not inhibit anyone from seeing me. Light a candle.' Myrna's hearing was then restored.

❖ THE AROMA OF MYRRH

The icon oozed oil for four days. Priests came and asked searching questions to see if it was a hoax. The priests sent for local officials and medical experts. The oil continued to flow from the icon and from Myrna's hands. When the clergy questioned Myrna they were astounded to learn that she said few prayers and attended Mass only on Wednesdays.

One day in early December, Myrna was praying in the company of a priest and a bishop. Suddenly she exclaimed, 'The Blessed Virgin has entered my soul!' Oil began to flow profusely from her palms and the bishop recognized the aroma as that of myrrh, used in anointing for sacramental healing. Soon crowds began to descend on the house and many cures were reported.

On 15 December, Myrna was praying in front of the icon with a huge crowd in attendance when suddenly she felt as if someone was pulling her towards the roof garden. There she knelt and, as she reported later, 'I looked up and saw the Blessed Virgin standing before me. She was shining all over, as if with jewels and gems. I was frightened and I ran away from there, screaming.' The whole family were afraid. Nicholas summoned a priest who was an expert in mystical theology and he taught Myrna to ask the Virgin directly what she would have her do.

✦ A WHITE BALL FILLED WITH LIGHT

Three days later, in the late evening, Myrna again felt drawn to the roof garden. Nicholas and some of his family and friends went with her. Myrna knelt in prayer and saw 'across the road, in a treetop, a white ball filled with light. It divided into two hemispheres and then vanished. I then saw the Lady standing, as it were, on a branch of the tree. She wore a blue cape and a white veil and she held a rosary.'

The vision drew close and said, 'Think of God, for God is here. I beseech you to do good to the wicked and do not ill-treat anyone. I have given you oil, but I also bring you something stronger than oil. Repent and proclaim my Son Jesus and you will be saved. Love one another.' The Virgin then requested a shrine, commanded all the people to pray

for unity among the Christian Churches and taught Myrna a new prayer:

> God saves me.
> Jesus enlightens me.
> The Holy Spirit is my life.
> Therefore I shall not fear.

The following day a father brought his paralysed son. As they prayed, oil flowed from the icon and again from Myrna's hands. She anointed the legs of the little boy, who began to walk for the first time in his life.

✦ A BLIND WOMAN HEALED

On 30 December the Patriarch Ignatius IV Hazim, having studied the events and questioned Myrna and Nicholas thoroughly, proclaimed the phenomena to be of supernatural origin. On 5 January 1983, a blind Muslim woman received her sight as she knelt in prayer before the icon. More than 120,000 people have witnessed the apparition of the miraculous oil, while a further million have seen it on video and many pilgrims have been healed.

The Blessed Virgin appeared frequently to Myrna and repeated her message of Christian unity. The family and some local priests set up an organization dedicated to carrying out Our Lady's wishes. They called themselves the Messengers of Unity and swore allegiance to the Catholic Bishop of Damascus, to emphasize the legitimate character of their group. They were anxious that the world should not regard them as a freakish sect. Their obedience has been wonderfully

Orthodox priests standing by an example of Byzantine iconography in a Syrian shrine

Myrna's hands. In 1987 Catholics and Orthodox set aside historical differences and celebrated Easter on the same day. They have promised to do so again in the year 2000.

On Good Friday 1987 Myrna received the stigmata, the marks of the wounds of Christ, in her palms. There is a film of the wounds and the marks made, as if by a crown of thorns, on her head. Myrna regularly suffers the Passion of Christ for three hours at a time – the period of our Lord's suffering on the Cross. She received visions of Jesus, who said, 'I am alpha and omega, the beginning and the end.'

The miraculous apparitions at Damascus are a sign of the unity which the Holy Mother desires for the whole Church – the same unity for which our Lord prayed shortly before his arrest. The wonder is that not only members of Christian denominations but also Jews and Muslims kneel to pray together at the house of Myrna and Nicholas Nazzour.

attested: when crowds turn up at Myrna's house and begin to spread tales of apparitions which do not have the Church's official backing, the oil does not flow either from the icon or from her palms.

✤ THE MARKS OF THE WOUNDS OF CHRIST

Remarkable results have arisen from the prayers for unity. On 18 June 1990, the Catholic Archbishop of Damascus testified that he had witnessed the oil flowing from

Information for Visitors

Location: The apparitions occurred at the home of Myrna Nazzour, in the Christian neighbourhood of Soufanieh. **Contact number:** TEL (963) 21 210 204 FAX (963) 21 219 031 **Times of Services:** Every 26 November, the anniversary of the first apparition, Masses are celebrated in churches all over Damascus followed in the evening by a prayer service and festivities at the house in Soufanieh.

THE BLACK MADONNA OF CANDELARIA

The Virgin came to visit us over the waves to the beach of Chimisay and we the Guanches placed her in the cave of Archinico.

FROM THE TRADITION OF THE KINGS OF TENERIFE, C. 1530

TENERIFE IS ONE of the principal Canary Islands in the Atlantic Ocean, 900 miles/1448 km south-west of Spain and 170 miles/274 km off the West African coast. There are no canaries in the Canary Islands: the name derives from the Latin for 'dog', *canis*, and dates from the first century when, according to the Roman writer Pliny, an African monarch sent out an expedition which returned bringing some huge dogs as souvenirs.

Candelaria is a picturesque village on the west coast. The sea wall is decorated by nine magnificent, huge statues of the Guanches, the ancient kings who ruled the island before the arrival of the Spanish in the fifteenth century.

At the end of the fourteenth century the Guanches found a wooden statue which had been washed up by the sea just south of Candelaria. Thinking that it might bring bad luck they tried to destroy it by throwing stones, but tradition says that they found themselves temporarily paralysed. After this experience they credited the image with

miraculous powers, though they had no idea whom it represented. It was a Black Madonna.

❖ A SHRINE ON THE OCEAN'S EDGE

The Guanches placed the statue in a cave, but during an exceptionally high tide it was washed out to sea again and lost. Meanwhile the Spanish had arrived and informed the islanders that the image was of the Blessed Virgin. A new statue was carved by Fernando Estevez in 1530 and this is the one currently housed in the Basilica de Nuestra Señora de la Candelaria in the town square.

The basilica is not huge, but stands imposingly on the edge of the square. It is the first thing you see when you descend from the surrounding hills and make your way through the narrow alleys between the old

OPPOSITE The beautiful interior of the shrine, dominated by a statue of Our Lady

houses. The interior, ablaze with light, is dominated by the statue of Our Lady, whose face wears the most tender expression imaginable.

On the Feasts of Our Lady and whenever there is an event such as a Confirmation or First Communion, the whole building is decorated with flowers. This basilica also houses Our Lady, Patroness of the Canary Islands, referred to as the Virgen de la Candelaria. Frequent pilgrimages and processions make their way to this stunningly beautiful shrine on the edge of the ocean. The highlight of the year is the great pilgrimage on 14–15 August to honour the Assumption. It is the tradition for all the college students on the islands to walk to Candelaria for this celebration, which is a religious devotion, but also something of a holy hike and a family picnic.

Information for Visitors

Location: on E coast S of Santa Cruz.
Contact Numbers: TEL (22) 500100 FAX (22) 502922. **Times of Services:** weekdays and Saturdays 8 a.m. and 6 p.m., Sundays 8 a.m., 10 a.m., 12 noon, 5 p.m. and 6 p.m.
Special Events: 2 February Festival of the Purification of the Blessed Virgin Mary, 15 August Feast of the Assumption.

So once again I went for my instruction
To him who took his beauty from Mary
As the morning star takes it from the sun.
Virgin Mother, daughter of your Son
Humbled and exalted beyond any other
  creature,
The settled end of the eternal plan.
In you there is mercy, in you there is pity,
In you magnificence, in you there is
Whatever goodness there ever was in
  creatures.

DANTE ALIGHIERI (1265–1321),
THE DIVINE COMEDY

—— UNITED STATES OF AMERICA ——

OUR LADY OF AMERICA

FOSTORIA, OHIO

O Holy Spirit, fire of everlasting love, consume me on the altar of Divine Charity that at the end of my life nothing may remain of me but that which bears the likeness of Christ.

OUR LADY TO SISTER MILDRED MARY NEUZIL, 1957

IN 1933 MILDRED MARY NEUZIL became a nun in the Order of Sisters of the Precious Blood in Fostoria. Sister Mildred gained an early reputation for humility and worked conscientiously as a domestic servant in four of the Order's houses. In 1938 she began to have deep spiritual experiences but did not speak of them; years later she wrote them down in her diary, although she has never revealed all the details.

While at her prayers on 8 November 1954 – the Feast of Mary, Our Shelter – Mildred heard the voice of the Blessed Virgin who said she would later appear and give urgent messages for the benefit of America and the whole world. On 25 September 1956, Mildred was in the corridor between the chapel and the refectory when she glimpsed a figure in a white dress with a blue sash. The figure announced herself as Our Lady of America. She said she was concerned for the young people of the country, and Mildred wrote down exactly what the vision said: 'My child, I entrust you with this message that you must make known to my children in America. I wish it to be the country dedicated to my purity. The wonders I work will be wonders of the soul. They must have faith and believe in my love for them. I desire that they be the children of my pure heart. I desire through my children of America to further the cause of faith and purity among all nations.'

✥ THE MEDAL OF OUR LADY OF AMERICA

The Blessed Virgin appeared several more times to Mildred that year. Our Lady looked to be wrapped in a glow of gentle light, and wore a white veil and a tall golden crown. She was barefoot and sometimes seemed to have clouds at her feet. In her right hand she held a lily, an emblem which matches the description in the Song of Songs: 'I am lily of the valley.' Sometimes Mildred glimpsed the Immaculate Heart, encircled by roses and pouring forth tongues of flame.

On 15 November, the Virgin asked Mildred to have a medal struck in her honour. This was to be inscribed 'Our Lady of America', and those who wore it were promised purity of heart and special grace from the Holy Mother and the Lord Jesus. These messages of comfort were in sharp contrast to dire warnings such as that issued in January 1957: 'My Son's patience will not last forever. Help me hold back his anger which is about to descend on sinful and ungrateful men. Suffering and anguish such as never before experienced is about to overtake mankind.'

Sister Mildred was not by nature or inclination a deep thinker. It is therefore remarkable testimony to the authenticity of her visions that the Virgin taught her some highly theological prayers concerning the mystery of the Holy Trinity and the very means of the Divine Indwelling.

✦ GREATER MIRACLES WILL BE PERFORMED IN AMERICA

Our Lady of America constantly stressed to Mildred the importance of the family as an instrument of God's grace and salvation. On her medal is emblazoned the coat of arms of all Christian families, who are encouraged to imitate the life of the Holy Family.

The Virgin told Mildred that America was not lower in the hierarchy of sacred places than Lourdes or Fatima. She said, 'Greater miracles will be performed in America. But I do not promise miracles of the body – rather of the soul.' The Virgin proclaimed that the USA was to be guardian of the world's peace. But as usual, the promise came with a caution: 'Unless the United States accepts and carries out faithfully the mandate given to it by heaven to lead the world to peace, there will come upon it and all nations a great havoc of war and incredible suffering. If however the US is faithful to this command from heaven yet fails in the pursuit of peace because the rest of the world will not accept or cooperate, then the US will not be burdened with the punishment about to fall.'

✦ A PLACE OF PILGRIMAGE

The Virgin requested a statue to be made and placed in the national shrine in Washington. The Holy Mother told Mildred, 'Thank my children on my behalf. Let it be made a place of pilgrimage. It will be a place of signs and wonders. I make this solemn promise: I will bless all those who by prayer, work or financial aid help to complete and beautify this shrine.'

Sister Mildred wrote a book entitled *Our Lady of America* which describes forty-two apparitions between 1954 and 1984.

Information for Visitors

Location: 40 miles/65 km S of Toledo.

OUR LADY OF PROMPT SUCCOUR
NEW ORLEANS

Under the title Our Lady of Prompt Succour, the Most Blessed Virgin has so often manifested her power and goodness that the religious have unbounded confidence in her.

FROM THE CHRONICLES OF THE URSULINE CONVENT, NEW ORLEANS

IN 1809 MOTHER ST MICHAEL was a highly regarded superior and teacher in the convent at Montpelier in France when she was asked by the Ursuline Order in New Orleans to go and live in America and to help educate Negroes and Native Americans. But her bishop was reluctant to let such an outstanding teacher leave his diocese and refused permission, saying that in any case the decision was a matter for the Pope. He reckoned that this would be the end of the affair because at that time the Pope was a prisoner of Napoleon.

Bur Mother St Michael was not so easily discouraged. She knelt in front of a statue of Our Lady and prayed, 'O Most Holy Mother, if you obtain a prompt and favourable reply to my request, I will honour you in New Orleans under the title of Our Lady of Prompt Succour.'

The letter to the Pope was posted on 19 March and the reply was received by Mother St Michael on 28 April. The Bishop joked that such a swift reply from the Vatican was itself a kind of miracle! He blessed the statue of the Virgin which Mother St Michael had had carved to take with her to New Orleans. She and her nuns arrived in America on 30 December 1810 and placed the statue in the convent chapel.

✧ THE BATTLE OF NEW ORLEANS

In 1812 there was a great fire in New Orleans and the nuns were ordered to evacuate their convent. Mother St Michael placed the statue on a window ledge facing the flames and prayed for deliverance. Amazingly, the wind changed and the fire which had been leaping towards the convent retreated and then died down completely.

On 9 December 1814 the British attempted to recolonize the United States and attacked New Orleans in small boats. A well-trained detachment of twenty thousand faced a ragged collection of American volunteers numbering fewer than seven thousand. The US army was led by General Andrew Jackson.

The women of the city processed to the convent of the Ursulines and prayed before the statue of Our Lady. Next day the British were defeated and the American forces

SHRINES OF OUR LADY

suffered remarkably few casualties. This astonishing victory was credited to the intercession of the Blessed Virgin. General Jackson went in person to the Ursuline convent to offer thanks.

❖ THE SHRINE TODAY

Every year on 8 January Mass is said in gratitude for the deliverance of New Orleans. In November 1895 Pope Leo XIII ordered that the statue of Our Lady should be crowned. In 1928 the Virgin was declared Our Lady of Prompt Succour, and the Patroness of New Orleans and the state of Louisiana.

Visitors to the shrine can see the original miraculous statue above the main altar. They can listen to the story of Mother St Michael and the statue, and see the five stained-glass windows which depict events in the life of the Blessed Virgin.

Information for Visitors

Location: New Orleans is a city and river port in Louisiana at the mouth of the Mississippi on the Gulf of Mexico. The shrine is to be found at 2635 State Street.
Contact Numbers: TEL (504) 866 1472 FAX (504) 866 8300. **Times of Services:** Sunday: 9.30 a.m.; Saturday: 11.30 a.m.; Monday to Friday: 7 a.m. or 5.15 p.m. (times vary). A Solemn Mass of Thanksgiving on Our Lady's Feast 8 January at 3 p.m. First Monday of each month: Prayers for Peace 1 p.m.-2 p.m.; Peace Mass 7 p.m. Additional services can be held for pilgrims on request.
Special events: The Patronal Festival is held on 15 January.

OUR LADY OF SCOTTSDALE
ARIZONA

Love one another always. Love all of different faiths. Never refuse anyone your love, for all belong to the Father. Never condemn. Always, always love. Be patient and peaceful children.
OUR LADY TO GIANNA TALONE, 28 DECEMBER 1989

ARIZONA CONTAINS some of the most starkly spectacular landscapes in the United States. Scottsdale is in the Valley of the Sun, a huge flat strip of desert ringed by red-rock mountains. In summer the temperature can rise to 35 degrees centigrade.

In June 1987 Father Jack Spaulding, parish priest of the Maria Goretti Church in Scottsdale, visited Medjugorje (see p. 41) with some parishioners including twenty-three-year-old Mary Coak, who turned passionately to the Christian faith during this pilgrimage. The following year another woman, Gianna Talone, who went on a visit to Medjugorje organized by Father Spaulding, was spiritually informed that she would 'play a significant part in the Holy Mother's grand plan'.

❖ WILL YOU GIVE EVERYTHING TO ME?

Father Spaulding had set up a prayer group dedicated to Our Lady. Gianna Talone, a member of this group, heard the Blessed Virgin say to her on 14 July 1988, 'Open your heart to Jesus. He wants to fill you with his grace. Pray!'

Other members too heard the voice of the Virgin and confided their experiences to Father Spaulding. Wendy Nelson first heard a divine voice in 1987. It said, 'Will you give everything to me?' Wendy became a lay helper at the Mission of Charity Congregation in Phoenix.

Gianna received her first vision on 19 December 1989. Then several members of the group – they became known as 'The Six' – experienced apparitions. Annie Ross observed on the evening of 28 December 1989, as Our Lady 'stepped out' of her statue

Our Lady of Scottsdale

in the Maria Goretti Church, 'She was not as she is in the statue itself, but a figure all glowing. She is young and slim with dark hair and blue eyes. She dresses in white and wears a veil. Our Lady is so beautiful that her appearance cannot be described in human language.'

Gianna has also reported visions of Our Lord in which he has given her lessons in the spiritual life. Father Spaulding was sometimes said to deliver homilies put directly into his mouth by the Blessed Virgin as an example of inspired supernatural utterance.

Week after week the visionaries fell into ecstatic trances during the Rosary and Holy Mass. Our Lady taught the visionaries simple prayers such as:

> Jesus, I adore you.
> I hope and trust in you.
> In you is all my faith.
> In you alone all things are possible
> And you are the living God.

❖ PROTECTION AGAINST EVIL DEVICES

Gianna in particular has suffered on account of her visions. She was in great pain during Lent 1989 and is regularly disturbed at night by physical assaults from the Devil, who has bruised and scarred her. She has lived a troubled life since her first vision. Her marriage was annulled, though she has remarried and moved to Maryland where she continues to receive visions and divine instructions.

When the first accounts of healing and blessings began to emerge from Scottsdale, Bishop Thomas O'Brien of the diocese of Phoenix set up a commission of investigation which reported that 'The messages are explicable within the range of ordinary human experience but we do not think there are any hoaxes or that there ever was any intention to deceive.' Father René Laurentin, a Marian authority who has also written about Argentinian apparitions, has talked at length with those who claimed to receive visions and has declared himself impressed by their sincerity and holiness of life.

The messages received by the visionaries were commands from the Virgin for an increase in family affection: 'Begin by loving your family. Love one another. And take care, for the Devil constantly strives to cause division and disrupt peace and unity in the whole world. Therefore, join together in love and you will have the shield you need to protect you against his evil devices.'

Information for Visitors

Location: 22 miles/14 km from Phoenix.
Contact Numbers: Tel (602) 257 0030
Fax (602) 258 3425. **Times of Services:**
Daily Mass 8 a.m., 5.30 p.m.; Our Lady's
Prayer Group each Thursday at 7 p.m.

AMERICA'S NATIONAL SHRINE
WASHINGTON DC

Our Lady is true Patroness of America. She has been so from the first. The flagship of Christopher Columbus was the Santa Maria.

FROM THE MAGAZINE *MARY'S SHRINE*

THE PROPOSAL for a national shrine for the United States was first suggested by the Reverend J.J. Aboulin of Detroit in 1914. Pope Pius X approved the scheme and said, 'It is most desirable that all Catholics should promptly and generously contribute towards the happy completion of this work.' The Reverend Bernard McKenna was appointed Shrine Secretary and the magazine *Salve Regina* was launched to publicize the project.

❖ A MAJESTIC BUILDING

In 1919 the new Pope, Benedict XV, declared that the work should be pursued with vigour. He promised a mosaic copy of the seventeenth-century Spanish painter Murillo's painting *The Immaculate Conception* for the high altar. The Pope died before the gift was made, but his successor Pius XI decided to give a copy of the *Purissima Bionda* in the Prado in Madrid. A site near the Catholic university was chosen.

A vast, domed building on a majestic scale was planned. The centrepiece was to be the Tower of Ivory, 100 metres tall, and the great

crypt would be the largest in the world. When the foundation stone was laid in 1920 the ceremony was attended by all the American bishops and diplomatic representatives from twenty-four countries.

To the east of the Mary Altar stands the Chapel of the Blessed Sacrament, and there are yet more altars depicting the Mysteries of the Rosary. The mosaic floor contains thirty-nine varieties of marble from all over the world. Fifty-eight granite and marble columns support the ceiling, and the largest of these have symbolic significance: the first one, a column from England, depicts prayer to Our Lady of Walsingham. There are also columns dedicated to Our Lady of Pilar, Spain; Our Lady of the Snows, Italy; Our Lady of Tinos, Greece; Our Lady of Bergen, Norway; Our Lady of Chartres, France and many more.

Unfortunately, the Wall Street crash of 1929 halted all progress on the building. In 1946 a new appeal was opened and the aim was to raise $1 million each year. Work was resumed in 1954 and the church was dedicated by Cardinal Spellman on 20 November 1959.

The National Shrine of the Immaculate

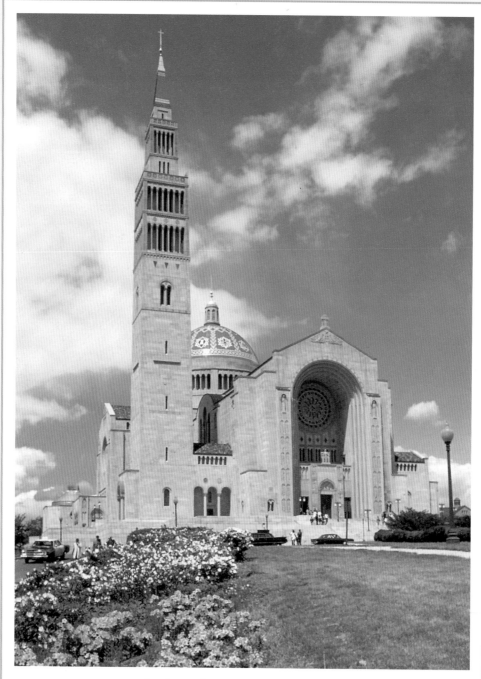

The Shrine of the Immaculate Conception

Conception is the seventh largest religious building in the world and the largest Catholic church in the western hemisphere. Able to accommodate six thousand worshippers, it was designated a basilica in 1990 by Pope John Paul II.

❖ CHURCHES WITHIN A CHURCH

The great National Shrine is composed of many churches within a church. Next to the Founder's Chapel is the Chapel of Pope Pius X, known as the Pope of the Rosary because he lowered the age at which children were allowed to receive First Communion. Across Memorial Hall is the Eastern Rite Chapel donated by the Byzantine-Ruthenian diocese of the USA. Don't miss the wonderful icons by the gates. A mosaic on a side wall depicts the emigration from eastern Europe to the coalmines in the USA, and the Pittsburgh skyline with its smokestacks.

Completed in 1997 was the Chapel of Our Mother of Africa, containing a bronze statue of the Madonna and Child. Directly outside Crypt Church is the Hall of American Saints and there are sculptures of two of them: St Elizabeth Ann Seton and St Francis Xavier Cambrini. Inside the Crypt Church itself is the Mary Memorial Altar, dedicated to Our Lady of the Catacombs and funded by thirty thousand women named Mary. The crypt features the largest masonry arch in the world. The Chapel of Our Lady of Lourdes contains a statue of the Virgin in a niche behind the altar. The words 'I am the Immaculate Conception' are carved into the Chapel's arch.

Near the altar is a stone from St Joan of Arc's prison cell. The Chapel of Our Lady of Czestochowa contains a reproduction of the famous Black Madonna and was a gift from Polish parishes in 1964.

In the north apse there is a massive mosaic of Christ in Majesty, one of the largest images of Our Lord in the world. Christ's face alone is over two metres in diameter. At his feet are nine angels. Really the National Shrine is like America itself – vast and cosmopolitan, containing images and representations of cultures and peoples worldwide who have found a new home in this great country.

There is a constant cycle of services and devotions every day and pilgrims are directed to particular 'churches within the church' where they may hear Mass in their own languages.

Information for Visitors

Location: Michigan Avenue, in NE Washington DC. **Contact Numbers:** TEL (202) 526 8300 FAX (202) 526 8313. **Times of Services:** The Great Upper Church: Saturday Vigil 5.15 p.m., Sundays 9 a.m., 10.30 a.m., 12 noon and 4.30 p.m. The Crypt Church: Sundays 7.30 a.m. and 1.30 p.m. (Latin), weekdays 7 a.m., 7.30 a.m., 8 a.m., 8.30 a.m., 12 noon and 5.30 p.m. Holy Days Vigil Mass 5.30 p.m., Mass 7 a.m., 7.30 a.m., 8 a.m., 8.30 a.m., 10 a.m., 12 noon and 5.30 p.m.

— WALES —

OUR LADY OF FATIMA

BALA, GWYNEDD

We must build a church to Our Lady of Fatima on the site of this fish and chip shop in Bala.
FATHER JAMES KOENEN TO HIS PARISHIONERS, APRIL 1946

THOUSANDS OF holidaymakers go each year to Lake Bala in the lee of the Cambrian mountains in North Wales. The scenery is spectacular: majestic hills and vast, serene stretches of water — what the musician Leonard Bernstein once described as 'Beethoven country'. The market town of Bala has also become a popular tourist resort.

Wales is a Protestant stronghold with Baptist chapels and Methodist churches on every street corner. Catholicism declined rapidly here after the Reformation when persecution of its devotees was particularly severe. It was reported in 1773 that there were only seven priests in the whole country.

In 1937 the Poor Sisters of Nazareth opened a convent at Llanycil, a village a few miles from Bala. Their father confessor lived in Bala where there was no Catholic church at all, so a building was needed. But the people were poor and there was no property available. The rootless little congregation prayed to the Blessed Virgin and vowed that, if she would provide them with a church, they would dedicate it to Our Lady of Fatima.

Within a few months an affordable property became available in the town's main street — a fish and chip shop! But the new priest, Father Koenen, would not be deterred and, largely thanks to his energy, the shop was purchased. For a time he worked almost single-handedly trying to convert the kitchen and disused stables.

❖ A BOLD PRIEST

Francis Leach, a Cambridge architect, then drew up plans for an altar and chancel-rail, and the walls were strengthened and restored. Pews were obtained from a redundant Methodist church and someone donated an old font. Father Koenen was bold enough to contact the authorities at Fatima (see p. 139) and tell them of his plans: Ferreira Thedun, sculptor of the statue of Our Lady of Fatima, agreed to carve the altar crucifix.

The church was consecrated in 1948 by the Diocesan Bishop of Menevia, North Wales, a ceremony attended by the Portuguese Vice-Consul and many prominent Catholics from England, Wales and Ireland. This was the first church in the world to be named after that of Our Lady of Fatima. The affair was enhanced by the presence of an internationally famous choir from Bologna who were taking part in the great annual Welsh cultural event known as the Eisteddfod.

A copy of the statue of Our Lady in Cova da Iria, the valley near to Fatima, was carved, then blessed by the Bishop of Leiria, the diocese in which Fatima is located. Many gave gifts of gold and precious stones for the crown. The statue arrived in an open-top car which stopped a little way short so that the statue could be carried in procession to the church in the main street. It was a tremendous event to happen in Protestant Wales.

The statue at Bala is a copy of Our Lady in Cova da Iria, Fatima

❖ CANDLE-LIT PROCESSIONS

Pilgrimages soon began and the little shrine became a highly popular place of devotion. On Whit Monday in 1961, four thousand pilgrims for world peace arrived. The church can accommodate scarcely more than two hundred worshippers, so when there is a large pilgrimage the faithful form a queue which in the evening becomes a candle-lit procession. Away from the main street is a large guest house which accommodates pilgrims and is the setting for vast open-air Masses.

The shrine of Our Lady at Bala celebrated its Golden Jubilee in 1998. The village itself is very small and only about forty catholics live there. Many pilgrimages are welcomed throughout the year and parties of visitors are given every assistance to find meals and accommodation by the Pilgrimage Director. It is a good idea to phone him if you are planning a visit (see below).

There is a special commemoration of Our Lady of Fatima on 13 May.

Information for Visitors

Location: by Lake Bala on A494. **Contact Number:** TEL (01678) 520 441 (Pilgrimage Director (01678) 520390). **Times of Services:** Sunday: 9 a.m., Monday – Saturday: 10 a.m. Eucharistic Service.

OUR LADY OF THE TAPER
CEREDIGION

At cock-crow a woman will descend from the vault of the choir, bearing a taper which she must present to the Bishop. When he has received it, he must drop some of the wax into jars of water, which he will then give to the sick, and they shall be cured.

FROM THE LEGEND OF OUR LADY OF THE TAPER

A PRIORY WAS established at Ceredigion (Cardigan in the English spelling) in 1111, and in those days churches associated with the priory were variously dedicated to the Holy Trinity, St Peter and St Mary. In 1539 the priory was suppressed and its properties confiscated by Henry VIII. Catholics regard the last Prior, William Barlow, as something of a traitor. He was nicknamed 'The Weathercock Reformer', for he willingly cooperated in the dissolution and was rewarded for his complicity by being made Protestant Bishop of St David's.

❖ THE LIGHT OF THE WORLD

Also at Ceredigion was the shrine of Our Lady of the Taper, the most visited Marian shrine in Wales at that time.

The statue of the seated Virgin was found, according to legend, beside the River Teifi, bearing a lit taper. The local people installed it in the church but it would not remain there and miraculously returned to its original place by the river. So the townspeople built another church by the water and dedicated it to Our Lady of the Taper.

Another tradition declares that the statue of Our Lady, having been spared the desecrations of the dissolution, was discovered in the church by Queen Elizabeth I who commanded that it should be thrown back into the River Teifi. The statue was the only image of the Virgin in England to represent Our Lady holding a taper. The symbolism of candles is, of course, very ancient in the Christian faith, representing to all people Jesus Christ, the Light of the World.

At the end of the nineteenth century, exiled Breton monks made their home in Wales where they were encouraged in missionary work by Bishop Mostyn of Cardiff. These Benedictines were welcomed in Wales because of their willingness to speak the Welsh language.

The monks discovered benefactresses in the Misses Lascelles, wealthy ladies who requested them to say Mass at their home each month. The sisters bought some land in 1904 and commissioned the building of a monastery,

The new bronze statue
of Our Lady of the Taper

but after the First World War it was sold and the monks returned to Brittany.

In 1926 the Bishop of Menevia asked the Carmelite nuns of Notting Hill, London, to establish themselves in Wales. The Carmelites were well connected with wealthy Catholic lay people and one of these, a Miss Emerson, bought land and property in the area and enabled the nuns to establish an enclosed Order at Bridell House just outside Ceredigion. She also purchased a large house in the town which was adapted to provide a church and presbytery. The church was dedicated in 1930 to Our Lady of Sorrow.

❖ OUR LADY ENTHRONED

Plans were eventually made to restore the original shrine, and a statue was commissioned from Dom Vincent Dapre of Farnborough Abbey in Hampshire. It featured Our Lady seated upon a throne with her feet on a footstool. The Christ Child was represented sitting in her lap and her luxuriant hair fell over her shoulders. In her right hand she held a massive taper supported by an arm of the throne.

As befits the National Shrine of Wales it was endowed with precious gifts, including a relic of Pope Pius X donated during the period when his canonization was being promoted by the Church. The first Mass in honour of Our Lady of the Taper was celebrated on 2 February, Candlemas Day, in the Marian Year 1954. Pilgrims started to arrive from Wales and beyond.

The statue of Our Lady of the Taper was blessed in Westminster Cathedral on the Sunday after Easter 1956 by Cardinal Griffin. From Westminster, the image was solemnly transported to Wrexham Pro-Cathedral to begin a six weeks' tour of all the Catholic parishes in Wales. Fittingly, the last day of this grand procession saw the statue arrive at the Chapel of Bridell House Convent. With great pomp and ceremony Our Lady of the Taper was enthroned in the new church at Ceredigion on 26 May 1956.

A further new church was completed in 1970, with a glass rear wall to allow for the overflow of pilgrims to participate in the services. On the wall is a Flemish tapestry symbolizing the sky, the earth, the sea and the pilgrim path which leads to Wales, all surrounded by the glow of candle light.

The 1956 statue did not prove durable and it was decided to commission a new one in bronze. This was blessed in 1986 and Ceredigion was designated the Welsh National Shrine of Our Lady. It is a beautiful crowned bronze image on a stone plinth. The Virgin's left arm is placed around the Christ Child, who sits on her knee. In her right hand she holds a candlestick. The Infant's expression is naturalistic, and he is robed and crowned in the same style as his mother.

On Pentecost Sunday, 18 May 1986, it was solemnly installed in its permanent home in the Shrine Chapel. A taper blessed by Pope John Paul II was placed in its hand and lit. A special message signed personally by the Holy Father was read out in the presence of over four thousand pilgrims.

Recently, the ruins of an old slipper chapel were discovered from which pilgrims used to walk barefoot to the shrine. This custom has been revived by local schoolchildren who can be seen, without shoes and socks, walking to the shrine to say their Rosaries on the great Feast Days of Our Lady.

Every year on St David's Day, 1 March, there is a pilgrimage in honour of the Patron Saint of Wales.

There is also a pilgrimage of reparation and consecration on a Saturday in July.

Information for Visitors

Location: on A487 on coast of W Wales.
Contact Number: TEL (01239) 612615.
Times of Services: Monday 11 a.m.; Tuesday–Friday 9.30 a.m.; Saturday 10.30 a.m. and 6.30 p.m.; Sunday 9.30 a.m.

USEFUL ADDRESSES

MARIAN SOCIETIES IN THE U.S.

May All Respond Yes
(M.A.R.Y. Ministries)
Ann Ross Fitch
P.O. Box 1982
Scottsdale, AZ 85252-1982
602-443-1112

MIR Center of San Francisco
P.O. Box 460354
San Francisco, CA 94146-0354
415-585-4749

Our Lady Queen of the Angels Peace Center
Terri and Norman Tanis
10009 Jovita Ave.
Los Angeles, CA 91311-3938
818-886-1318

Center for Peace—Denver
Jo Ann and Ed Langfield
1638 S. Rosemary St.
Denver, CO 80231-2604
303-755-7070

The National Shrine of the Immaculate
Conception
Fourth St. and Michigan Ave., N.E.
Washington, DC 20017
202-526-8300

Florida Center for Peace
Luis Siman
P.O. Box 431306
Miami, FL 33143
800-238-5538
305-666-5000

Chicago Marian Center
Kathleen Long
1847 West Estes
Chicago, IL 60626
800-446-PRAY (7729)
312-973-0739
Fax: 312-973-0788

National Votive Shrine of Our Lady of Prompt Succor
Rev. Douglas Brougher
2635 State St.
New Orleans, LA 70118
504-866-1472

Marian Renewal Ministry
Fr. Al Winshman, S.J.
300 Newbury St.
Boston, MA 02115-2805
617-266-7510

United Apostolates of Jesus and Mary
Karen Ruberto / Rudy Motard
54 Salvation Ridge St.
St. Louis, MO 63026
314-861-0021
motord@wuche.wust.edu

Saint Francis Cabrini Chapel
701 Fort Washington Ave.
New York, NY 10040
212-923-3536

Medjugorje in America
Celine Dudley
387 E. 149th St.
Cleveland, OH 44116
216-531-7118

**The Grotto National Sanctuary of
Our Sorrowful Mother**
Sr. Ruth Arnott
8840 NE Skidmore St.
P.O. Box 20008
Portland, OR 97220
503-254-7371

Center for the Queen of Peace
Rafael Brom
3350 Highway 6
Suite 412
Houston, TX 77478
800-695-952

Center for Peace – West
James P. Yancey
P.O. Box 55748
Seattle, WA 98155
206-743-6370
Fax: 206-481-3110

BIBLIOGRAPHY

An Appeal from Mary in Argentina, Rene Laurentin, McCrimmon Publishing Co, 1995

Dictionary of Mary, produced by the Catholic Book Publishing Company, 1985

Famous Shrines of Our Lady (3 vols), Peter Heintz, Gabriel Press, 1993

Meetings With Mary, Janice T. Connell, Random House (hardback), 1996, and Virgin Books (paperback), 1996

Miraculous Images of Our Lady, J. J. Cruz, Tan Books, 1993

Praying With Mary, Janice T. Connell, Harper Collins, 1997

Those Who Saw Her, Catherine M. Odell, Our Sunday Visitor Publishing Division, 1986

The Visions of the Children: The Apparitions of the Blessed Mother at Medjugorje, Janice T. Connell, St Martin's Press, 1992

Visions of Mary, Peter Eicher, Avon Books, 1996

INDEX